TAGORE AND EDUCATION FOR SOCIAL CHANGE

TAGORE AND EDUCATION FOR SOCIAL CHANGE

MOHIT CHAKRABARTI

GYAN

Tagore and Education for Social Change

ISBN : 978-81-212-0436-1

First Published 1985, reprint 2013 in India by
Gyan Publishing House
23, Main Ansari Road, Daryaganj,
New Delhi - 110002
Phones : 23282060, 23261060

Fax : (011) 23285914
E-mail: books@gyanbooks.com
website: gyanbooks.com

Printed at : Sagar Color Scan, New Delhi.

CONTENTS

Preface

Education is a quest within. It is a quest for inward excellence. What is that inward excellence ? What are the components that amply contribute to that inward excellence ? How to indentify them ? What are their relations with social consiousness ? How does education make a happy fusion between the individual and the society ? As an unparalleled social thinker, Rabindranath Tagore delves deep into the role of education for social change and negotiates all these queries with astonishing marvels of innovative experiments.

Quite often misinterpreted as a genius alien to down-to-earth experiences of the masses in the society, Rabindranath practically plunges a crusade against all constraints of dissemination of mass education to bring about a radical, fruitful, sustained and meaningful social change to justify his humble but yet to be warmly accepted submission : *Ami tomaderi lok,* I am truly yours. "Mass Education and Social Change : Tagorean Strategies" is a pointer to this.

Not merely social change for the sake of change alone but also for aesthetic excellence towards which education, as Rabindranath for the first time makes us aware, should be carefully and cautiously directed. This has a two-fold avenue of challenge : one, to ignore bare emotionalism and sentimentalism violently nursed by the protagonists of 'national' education and the second, to introduce a serene dedication and devotion to Truth, Beauty and Goodness in any programme of education for social change. "Education for Socio-Aesthetic Excellence : Tagorean Guidelines" is an intensive study on this end in view.

The much nagging and delicate problem of education for

promotion of social cohesion has more often than not been either brushed aside or given lukewarm response in plans and programmes of education, and the role of education to negotiate this burning problem even now rests assured in firefighting operation only leaving aside intricate problems of the society awaiting immediate and longterm solutions through purposeful and multi-dimensional approach to education. "Education for Promotion of Social Cohesion : Tagorean Perspectives" is a study that might provoke experimentations anew towards this direction.

"Education for Socio-Mystic Fulfilment : Tagorean Piognance" and "Education of Creative Appreciation and Social Change : Tagorean Experiments" might invite serious thoughts of everyone deeply concerned with education for social change.

While making an indepth study on the educational thoughts and experiments of Rabindranath Tagore, I have been greatly inspired by the significant words of encouragement and probing vision of Professor Sabyasachi Bhattacharya, Vice-Chancellor, Visva-Bharați University, Santiniketan. I humbly dedicate my book to him as a token of my reverence.

Togore's social thinking re-thought and re-translated into action is humanity reborn, re-evaluated and revitalized. If the book appeals to the revered readers interested in Tagorean viewpoints and guidelines on education for social change and rewards me with their valued criticism I would remain serenely grateful.

MOHIT CHAKRABARTI

Seemantika

Visva-Bharati University

Santiniketan

1

EDUCATION FOR SOCIAL AWARENESS

TAGOREAN VIEWPOINTS

Education is always an adventure thrilling, lively and joyous It is a journey within, endless but interesting, ardu ous but promising. It takes into account every pattern of human endeavour, be it little or great. The eternal askance of man within is the askance of consciousness individual as well as social. To be in the cocoon of oneself is not necessarily to be lost in oneself, for the great awakening of oneself is always inherent in the spirit of extinction of oneself for one and all. This extinction is a beckoning of one's being social. Education starts with this promise of making oneself social through extinction of the little 'I' that craves for prominence.

An apostle of social reincarnation, Rabindranath Tagore

highlights education for inner social consciousness. He asserts more on being social than on being an individual, for he believes that an individual is meaningless unless he is of any real use to the society to which he belongs. An individual is also meaningless if he fails to ignite his inner worth to be justified to his individuality. The urge within is to be bloomed in pure and perfect efflorescence. How can an individual be pure and perfect unless he is inspired within himself with the great human sensibility: *Vasudhaiva Kutumvakam* — let all the world be in kinship with me?

Brought up in affluence and dissociated from the experience of social disparites in boyhood, Tagore had an agonized heart that pined for having a closer view of society in and around him. The beckonings of the All Beautiful are in perfect unison of all in the eternal muse of togetherness:

Oder sathe melao jara charay tomer dhenu,
Tomar naame vajaay jara venu.
Pasan diye vandha ghate ei-je kolahaler hat.,
Kena ami kiser lobhe enu.
Ki daak daki · vaner pataguli, kaar isara-triner anguly;
Pranesh amar lilabhare khelen praner khelaghare
Pakhir mukhe ei-je khavar penu.

Unite me with them who tend your cows,
Who play on the flute in your name.
On the stone-built bank, in this melee of chaos
Why and for what attraction did I come.
What's the call of the forest leaves, whose beckonings are thro the grass
The God of my heart does play in the playhouse of the heart with all mysteries,
This is the news that from the mouth of birds did I receive.

Rabindranath Tagore : *Songs, Rabindra-Rachanavali,* Government of West Bengal, Calcutta. 1980. Vol.II. No. 900, p. 373.

[Translated by me.

More often misunderstood than not, Tagore has an aching heart for the toiling millions who work untiringly and eke out their livelihood in bareness and simplicity. Here is a realistic picture of the society as portrayed in touching words:

> Endlessly do they
> Pull on cars, holds on the steering.
> From field to field do they
> Sow seeds, reap ripe paddy.
> They work
> In cities and fields.
> The septre tumbles down, no sound emerges from the drum of war,
> The tower of victory forgets like the dunce its meaning
> All the bloody eyes with bloodstained weapons in hands
> Remain wrapped in stories meant for children.
> They work
> In countries beyond countries
> In the sea-shores and river-banks of *Anga, Banga* and *Kalinga*
> In Punjab, Bombay and Gujarat.
> The roaring and the humming sounds
> By day and at night are enclasped and make the passing of the day enamoured.
> Sorrow and happiness, day and night
> The sounds of the great chanting of life do make

resonant.
On the remains of ruins of hundreds of empires
They work.

—— Rabindranath Tagore: *Arogya (Convalescence), Rabindra Rachanavali,* Government of West Bengal, Calcutta. 1980. Vol. III. No. 10. p. 828.

[Translated by me.

Rabindranath always believes that education is always a challenge within. It is a sort or a means for social transcendence– a march from what man is to what man should be. It is, indeed, the perfect vehicle for beyonding of man. What may be called Tagorean naturalism in education is entirely harmonized with his educational socialism. His own vision of an ideal institution based on the principle of social consciousness may be recalled:

We should have the gift to be
natural with nature and human
with human society.

—— Rabindranath Tagore: "A Poet's School", *Visva- Bharati Bulletin,* Visva-Bharati, Santiniketan. No. 9. p. 6.

Highly sensitive as he is, Tagore has the social kinship with the living drama of human life that often aches him with the poignance of vision. He comes nearer to the people of the society not externally but introspectively in course of his critical and creative endeavour. A sense of nostalgia so touching and picturesque spreads the vast social canvas in the panorama of life in all its diversities through the incomparable expression of a great seer of humanity. Even in his waning years, he lovingly recalls the simple events very realistically:

At a distance, the bell rings
These clamorous self-announcement piercing the
sky of the town
From the mind disappeared
In the heated sum of *Magh*, flashed in the
eyes without reason the picture
That on the edge of the way of life not very
visible remained,
Knitting the hamlets the meadowy path has
towards the distance gone
Crossing o'er the embankments of the river
The ancient shade of the *Asatha* tree,
The people are seated in the hope of
crossing the river
Keeping the marketing producers nearby.
In the tinplate rooms of the *gunge*
Piles of pitchers with condensed juice of
sugar-candies.
The dogs of the locality lick by being a prey
to perfume.
Flies crowd.
On the roads, carts put upside down
Are burdened with jute
Weighing goes on aloud by pulling the bags
one by one.
In the courtyard of the storehouse
The oxen bereft of yokes
Squander on the green edge of the road by
eating grass,
Beat on the back by hairy fan of the tail
Heaps of mustard seeds are there
Waiting for storage in the corn-containers.
The fishing boats come on the banks,
The fisherwomen have assembled with buckets on
their waists:
Overhead the kite flies. The business-boats are bound
side by side on the sloping.

sandbanks.
Sitting in the sun, the oarsmen are weaving nets on the roof of tin sheeds
The ploughman floats on swimming by clasping the neck of the buffalo
Towards the other side in paddy fields.
Beyond the forest, the apex of the temple not far away
Is shining in the morning sunlight.
Beyond the visible side of the field, the train runs on
With gradually feeble
Whistling lines of sound drawn on the canvas of ether
Spreading the smoke behind.
As a mark of the long flag of victory of winning the distance.
I remember, that's nothing, long long ago,
It was midnight.
The boats were anchored on the bank of the Ganges
The shining water in moonlight.
The images of shadow consolidated on the edges of the forest untrembled
The flame of the lamp is rarely seen thro' the forest.
Suddenly I awoke
In the soundless midnight sky
The young voice in the song echoes,
The lean boat sweepingly runs in the ebb-tide current
In an instant it vanished:
Mystery reigned in the sombre forest on the two banks:
The image of the quiet night dressed with the crown of the moon
In the seat of the humbled slumber did speechless remain.
The western bank of the Ganges, the residence is at the fag end of the town.
The long stretched sand bank
Beneath the vacant sky as if makes a commentary on futility.

Cows graze to and fro in the empty field of maize
From the creepers of water-melon
The farmer-boy drives with a stick the goats away
Somewhere, again, the rural woman
Roams in search of spinach with basket on her waist.
Off beside river-line far away
A group of oarsmen with bowed down backs, tired
movements, pulling the ropes.
No more freshness prevails in the water or land
all day long.
In the nearby garden, the *golakchanpa* is unendeared
The old great *neem* tree with seat prepared below
The aristocratic shadow of hers deep and serene.
Storks take shelter at nignt there.
The water pulled out of the well
All day long makes rippling sounds in its course
through the drains
To instill life in the fields of oats.
Bhajia crushes oats in a wheel-crusher
With her brass-bangled hands.
The stretched tune the noon enchants.
This on-the-way scene
Transitory as it was
In the distant domain of consciousness,
Up that comes in the mind today.
All these pictures discarded
The latest pain of separation of life
Bring forth in the mind with the sound of the distant
bell.

—— Rabindranath Tagore: *Arogya* (Convalescence), *Rabindra-Rachanvali*, Government of West Bengal, Calcutta. 1980.Vol.II. No. 4, pp. 823-825.

[Translated by me.

The simple social life of ordinary rural people who

have an intimate association with nature and the unsophisticated object of nature never averts Tagore's attention. He enters deep into every social panorama of life to drink the inner nectar of beauty and truth.

He looks introspectively to be a real partner to every social symbol of awareness as revealed in the day to day drama of human life.

A look back into the social history of man brings forth for the poet a mixed feeling of human values. For India, he has an agonised social sense of awareness which touches the very core of social sensibilities. And what remains save emptiness, *sans* vainglory ? The wheel of life makes a new beginning from typicalities of behavioural designs. A new chapter is welcomed to show man's march from time beyond time:

> Rowing through the flow of idle time
> The mind goes on looking towards emptiness
> The picture painted in shadow arrests the eyes
> in the path of that vast emptiness
> In groups, for time endless, so many people have
> gone
> In time long past
> In forceful speed of the pomp of victory.
> The groups of the Pathans have come
> with the greed of empire.
> The Moghuls have come.
> The wheels of the chariot of victory
> Have sped past the web of dust and the flag
> of victory
> Towards the avenue of emptiness do I look
> No trace of that do I find today.
> In that clear sky in the morn and in the eve
> The light of sunrise and sunset adorned from
> time to time.
> Once again in that abode of emptiness
> In groups have come

Thro iron-string avenue
In the chariot that believes in fire
The mighty English
Have exposed their power.
Know I that time would flow on even in
their avenue
To the endless would it sweep away the countrywide
dragnet of empire.
Know I that her soldiers carrying the burden of
commodities
Would leave no trace in the avenue of the
world of light
We see there in murmuring sounds
Endless crowd tread on
In diverse avenues and in different groups
From time beyond time in eternal human needs
In life and in death.

—— Rabindranath Tagore: *Convalescence* *(Arogya), Rabindra Rachanvali,* Government of West Bengal, Calcutta, 1980. Vol.III. No. 10. pp. 827-828.

[Translated by me.

The vast panorama of social awareness as Tagore portrays above, indicates the fact that he penetrates deep into the inner soul of human consciousness. The experience he receives of social transcendence from a fusion of humanism and social responsibilities goes a long way in the transcendence of social norms and values which suffer from multidimensional constraints. Consequently, he appeals for social and cultural synthesis and upholds the inherent spirit of such a desirable but yet neglected synthesis. A radical idea of history that suggests for a renovated approach thereto is, as he strongly advocates, the only way out. This can be further illustrated through his essay `*Chhatrasasantantra*'later translated and published in *The Modern Review,* April 1916:

> The history of man takes different shapes different countries. The history of India has also its specialities. From the very beginning of her history, we have been visualizing that this country is not meant for a particular nation or a particular civilization. Just as the Aryan civilization is true in this country, so is the Dravidian civilization. In this country, the Muslims are not less big than the Hindus. For this very reason, the very history of this country has, like an enormous meteor, become blurred with the vapour of clashes of diverse conflicts. We have been encountering the commotion of different forces in this history but we have not yet visualized the outcome of an undivided historical image. The distant cry of an eternally inseparable "I " out of this expanded vastness has not yet awakened.

—— Rabindranath Tagore: `*Chhatrasasantantra'Siksha,* Visva-Bharati, 1973. p. 165.

[Translated by me.

For an eternally inseparable "I" amid the infinite vastness of social awareness spread over the sea of humanity, Tagore wants to have a sound platform of education that caters to the history of human civilization. Such a platform would allow all entrants to social consciousness to be thrilled with the marvels of indigenous civilization. As a matter of fact, his exposition on the role of the university as a centre for dissemination of desirable social awareness serves as a genuine and invaluable reminder to regain the lost of social enrichment:

> There is no need for elaborate descrip-

tion on the origin of the university. What I want to say in general is: To protect and disseminate the special love, glory and responsibility felt by a particular country, a particular nation on the discipline naturally refers to the first creation of a university. The intention that is at the grass-root level of all creation is the outcome of that very will-force of the country. At the root of this intention lies the grandeur of power. That grandeur wants to express itself in continual spontaneity by grace: it cannot be dissuaded.

All civilized countries make the hospitality of erudition wide open for their own universities. One who has excess of wealth welcomes the guests. The host admits the universe in his own guest house. At Nalanda, India opened the institution for dissemination of her own knowledge for all the invitees of her own country and abroad. On that day she felt that she has so wealth in abundant qualities as to find her highest success in contributing to mankind. In most of the countries of the western continent this guest house of learning is existent. There is no difference between the native and the foreigner there. In the universal sphere of learning there, every man is reciprocally very own. In almost all parts of the society the barriers of dissociation are becoming insurmountable everyday. Only in this great pilgrimage of knowledge the invitation for mankind persisted. This is because to admit poverty and austerity in this sphere is the most alleviating factor of the self for a civilized race. The courtyard of the fortunate country is wide open towards the universe in this sphere.

—— Rabindranath Tagore: "*Visvavidyalayer Roop*" *Siksha*, Vishva-Bharati, 1973. pp. 207-208]

[Translated by me.

To bring about a certain cohesion in social awareness and social sensibilities in mankind is what Tagore considers to be one of the primary objectives of education. No fragmentation but unison of knowledge and experience derived from diverse social exposures accelerates excellence of man. True education adorns everything that brings forth social harmony and so like a dedicated social visionary, Tagore evaluates education in terms of delving deep into the core of human consciousness and unfolds the ideal avenue of social synchronization from the Indian perspective:

> Even the educated people of our country cry out at times: Whom do you call as your country? What is the special characteristic of our country? Where do you encounter it? Where did it exist? No answer can be found, because the proposition is so delicate, so wide that it cannot be negotiated by arguments alone. What with the English or with the French nobody can express in a single word what the special characteristic of his country is, and where it lies in its core. That is as true as life in the body but inaccessible like life in concept and idea. That enters from childhood amidst our knowledge, love and imagination through unmarked avenues and in diverse forms. That builds us intensively with diverse strength. That does not allow any difference between the past and the present. It is due to its grace that we are great and not disassociated. How shall we explain with two or three words this strength of yore adorned with diverse endeavour with a definition to a

dubious learner ?

There is an explicit answer to those who ask on the fundamental significance of India. The history of India would support that very answer. The only endeavour on the part of India for ever as visualized by me is to establish unity in difference, direct diverse avenues towards the same objectives and understand without doubt the one in the midst of legion as the core of the heart. The differences apparently felt are not to be destroyed but to be in possession of inherent unison.

To visualize this oneness and to make an endeavour for the dissemination of this oneness are very obvious for India. For this very trait on her part, she has remained in different for ever to national glory. This is because the idea of conflict lies at the root of national glory. Those who fail to feel the distant as the most distant heart and soul cannot consider the attainment of national glory to be the ultimate aim of life. The endeavour to establish oneself above others lies at the root of political achievement. To relate oneself to other and to try to make a synchronization between the diverse departments and conflicts within oneself this points towards religious and social development.

— Rabindranath Tagore: *"Bharatvarsa O Swadesh"*, *'Bharatvarser Itihas'*, *Rabindra-Rachanavali*, Government of West Bengal, Calcutta 1961. Vol. XII.p.1029.

[Translated by me.

For a global social understanding, Tagore rightly thinks that education should bring forth vastness in approach to the history of mankind. Every man is, therefore, a partner to all who strive for the understanding and appreciation of man as man. As soon as he strives, he is on the go for the march of mankind for greater social cohesion. The unison of global culture, tradition and values sees the dawn of reality. Perhaps from this definite approach to social awareness Tagore advocates for necessary emulation of social culture and values, traditions and heritage of the West. As he characteristically observes:

> I am observing that as there are the Aryans, the Dravidians, as the Muslims so are also the British. The real history of India is, therefore, not only our history but also the history of the British. Now we will have to see if these different parts of history are properly synchronized and the whole thing becomes a part of the living body. We have no ability to eliminate any of the parts. We could not leave the Muslims aside nor would we be able to leave the English. This is not due to the absence of physical strength, the very nature of the history is this. It is not the history of a particular nation but it is the chemical process of the history of humanity.

—— Rabindranath Tagore: " *Chhatrasasantantra*", *Siksha,* Visva-Bharati, 1973. p. 165.

To be aware of the chemical process of the history of humanity is to be aware of the broader social visions of mankind. Man today is an inseparable part of the global society and any progress of mankind cannot but be in close relation to the broader social development of global mankind. The vision of the universal brotherhood of mankind as Tagore visualizes and gives shape in his own educational experimentations at Santinikentan and Sriniketan is actually a re-orientation of education for efflorescence of social consciousness. Let bookish education-a craze even now tempering and bringing forth massacres in legion— be radically replaced by education for emancipation of social awareness. Let the education of being revolutionalize the heartland of true humanity. The indwelling light of Truth' of oneness of which man alone can boast is the genesis of joy and fulfilment of the prized outcome of a harmony of truth within and that of the society. Tagore's exposition brings out the point better:

> By the indwelling light of this truth, I know that the world to which I belong, and which consists of an endless series of movements, has an inner truth of its own which is one, and which gives reality to the innumerable facts we know about the universe. We realize this inner truth, we experience *Ananda*, Joy, for through Joy we discover the eternal harmony of our own reality.
>
> So often we ignore the real truth of a man and only deal with surface facts about him. The man who sells things to me is, for myself, a mere fact. The man whom I employ as my servant is a bundle of certain facts, all useful in the particular facts and circumstances of my life. Through such facts I find the satisfaction of many of my needs, but no joy. For joy comes only when we realize the harmony of the *Satyam*, or Truth, that is in us, with the *Satyam*, or Truth, that is in others, and, in this case, in my servant. But with regard to our loved ones, we are directly aware of the deeper truth which is constantly manifested through them in their outer life, because with them we more easily realize a

> mutual affinity. Their outer activity may hold no value for our own life's purposes. May it may even be a indrance. They have, however, an ultimate value for us in that they are, that they embody, an inner truth which is also within me.

—— Rabindranath Tagore: "The Philosophical Approach to Sriniketan" , incorporated in L.K. Elmhirst: *Rabindranath Tagore: Pioneer in Education,* Visva-Bharati 1961 p.86.

To feel within each'I' the inner pulse of every 'We' is the primary symbol of social awareness as Tagore encompasses in his theory of education for social consciousness. It is to discover the inner truth, the inner vision of unfolding true humanity. For such a purpose the role of the external life of a human being is to be synchronized with the internal life to ward off any inconsistencies whatsoever.

To fulfil the above objective of synchronization, Tagore essentially emphasized on education—living, pulsating, dynamic, down-to-earth. He emphasizes on a unison between education and life. Education dissociated from life as it is today is no education. It dissociates man from man, life from life. it does not allow anyone to cultivate the seeds of social awareness. Instead, it differentiate man from man and debases the desired goal of life to achieve truth and joy. The agonies of the soul pining for fulfillment of social effulgence deeply.move Tagore who believes in the infinite spirit of man to come out victorious in the struggle for social harmony. In his essay " *Sikshar Herpher* " (" Topsy-Turvy in Education ") he refers to the appalling alienation between man and society and prays for a social cohesion of consciousness:

> Being dissociated, man is becoming a failure. He cannot stand up strong by achieving an indivisible pattern of unity within himself.

He is not getting anything necessary for him within his reach at the appropriate point of time. There is a story. When a poor man would purchase winter garments by saving little by little during winter, the summer season would, in the meantime, step in. Again, when he would be able to procure light dresses by striving throughout the summer season, the early winter would set in. When, seeing his poverty the Almighty became merciful and wanted to bless him with a boon he said, 'Nothing more do I want, please do away with this topsy-turvy. If you make a slight correction so that I might receive garments of summer and winter at the appropriate time, I think my life would be meaningful'.

We have also the same prayer. If the differences are eliminated, we are contented. We have this appalling poverty because we are failing to make conformity between winter and garments for the winter, summer and garments for the summer. Otherwise everything we have. Now we pray for this boon to the Almighty: synchronize our appetite with food, clothes with seasons, ideas with language, and education with life. Our position is like :

Fish athirsty in water
arousing volleys of laughter.

Seeing that we have both water and thirst, the people of the world are laughing and tears are rolling down from our eyes. Only we are failing to drink.

—— Rabindranath Tagore: " *Siksher Herpher* ", *Siksha* Visva-Bharati, 1973 pp. 18-19.

[Translated by me.

How do these alarming inconsistencies thrive in humanity? Why is mankind gradually becoming a prey to affluence and a slave to utilitarianism ? Why is the hungry heart of an individual a victim to materialism ? The macabre joy of a mechanomaniac as an eroding man appears today, lies only in an exile to nowhere since greed and passivity mock at humanity.Whether man? Whither social awareness?

Nearly seventy years ago, Tagore wanted to make the global mankind aware of the perils of passivity and greed. That civilization cannot but identify the numerous ills prevalent in human beings is the forewarning that he again and again makes not because the world is to be passively ignored but essentially because man is becoming alienated both from men and within himself. He becomes a curious creature *sans* social awareness *sans* conjoint communicated caressed living. To be aware of the modern society, it might even now be appropriate to rethink on Tagore's views on civilization and the modern society:

> Civilization today caters for a whole population of gluttons. An intemperance which could safely have been tolerated in a few, has spread its contagion to the multitued. This universal greed, which now infects us all, is the cause of every kind of meanness, of cruelty and of lies in politics and commerce, and vitiates the whole human atmoshpere. A civilization which has attained such an unnatural appetite, must, for its continuing existence, depend upon numberless victims. These are being sought in those parts of the world where human flesh is cheap.

In Asia and Africa a bartering goes on through which the future hope and happiness of entire people is sold for the sake of providing some fastidious fashion with an endless supply of respectable rubbish.

The consequences of such a material and moral drain is made evident when one studies the condition manifested in the grossness of our cities and the physical and mental anaemia of the villages almost everywhere in the world. For cities inevitably have become important. The city represents energy and materials concentrated for the satisfaction of an exaggerated appetite, and this concentration is considered to be a symptom of civilization. The devastating process of such an abnormality cannot be carried on unless certainn parts of the social body conspire and organizeto feed upon the whole. This is suicidal; but before a gradual degeneracy ends in death, the disproportionate enlargement of the particular portion looks formidably great. It conceals the starved piller of the entire body. The illusion of wealth becomes evident because certain portions grow large on their robbery of the whole.

—— Rabindranath Tagore: Presidential Address under the auspices of the Visva-Bharati Sammilani at the Rammohan Library, Calcutta, July 28, 1922. Published as "Introduction to 'The Robbery of the Soul'" in L.K.Elmhirst: *Poet and Ploughman*, Visva-Bharati, Calcutta 1975, pp. 34-35.

Education dissociated from social awareness as it imparted in right earnest takes no interest in making newer avenues of unfolding inner consciousness. As a consequence, dishonesty creeps in every sphere of the society. The real `man' in man is ignored in education that betrays to be truly civilized. As a socio-cultural being, man cannot remain a silent sectator to blatant hypocrisy in the name of progress and civilization. This is, in fact, a course of dehumanization of man is sham socio-cultural change through miseducation. Tagore points towards this crisis of consiciousness as a social foreseer as follows:

> We do not feel slightly ashamed to admit that it is enough to go on maintaining the external status alone. We do not even hesitate to say that we can do whatever we would practically like to do but there is no harm if we do not admit it publicly. This type of practice in dishonesty is to be accepted by man under trying circumstances. This is because when your reverence has taken a different course, the people of the society do not feel ashamed by taking recourse to dishonest means in case the society stifles the conventions in the same place. As there are very few heroic personalities amongst people, this state of affairs goes on. Therefore, where the punishment for admitting truth in public is intolerably great, one cannot consider it to be a crime to take recourse to hypocrisy.

—— Rabindranath Tagore: " *Sikshavidhi* "—("Principles of Education"), *Siksha*. Visva-Bharati, 1973 p. 126.

[Translated by me.

To arrest the crisis of character of a marooned humanity is the first and foremost objective of any educational programme for human consciousness. For Rabindranath, it is the education for sympathy that should serve as continual guideline for education to bring about any social change. Apathy and ignorance, as he has most practically asserted, are the 'worst forms of bondage for man'. The education of sympathy for social awareness is long overdue. It is that education which opens wider avenues for socio-aesthetic unison of awareness. Tagore makes a characteristic exposure in this connection:

> When we received education of the West for the first time, the refrain that we had from that education is: ' No difference is there between man and man. Therefore, we were going to be grown up in such a way as we would be able to eliminate all our points of differences with the new teacher. Just at that time closing his books on religion the teacher said, 'There's so much difference between the East and the West, that there's no scope for overcoming that.
>
> Well, there is difference, and let there difference be. Diversities direct towards keeping good health. As heat and cold are not one and the same at every place, so the wind passes. Let the different ideals of civilization be successful from diverse manifestations. Then that would be a means of mutual exchange of education in that uniqueness.
>
> In fact, there are differences in civilization; that very diversity is which is desirable to the creator. The success of this diversity lies in mutual understanding with earnestness of enriched knowledge. The education and exercise that bar the doors of entrance to this indicate barbarities. And for this injustice and cruelty are created. What are the symptoms of true civilization? That is civilization which encompasses: He alone, who remains in all, knows all— *Sa Sarvajnah Sarvamavivesha* : knows all

> and enters inside all. The ideal which is in enmity with others is not an ideal at all.

—— Rabindranath Tagore: "*Samajbhed*" ("Differences in Society"), *Rabindra-Rachanavali,* Tagore Centenary Edition, Government of West Bengal, Calcutta, 1961 Vol. XII, pp. 1091-1095.

[Translated by me.

A conscious society, as Tagore emphasizes, is the outcome of education that eliminates all differences to foster civilization in the right perspective of good sense and sensibilities. It is a society that disseminates education for understanding *Satyam* - Truth - that allows the learner to see reality not merely outwardly but also introspectively. To accelerate the inner truth of life and society, Tagore wants everyone of us to evolve so that the society in which we live can be practically identified with the ideals of truth and knowledge. This may be termed as a concept of Tagore's vision of social awareness which serves as a basis of his social experiments at Sriniketan. As he observes,

> We are born conscious of one truth, which is for us the background to our knowledge of all other truths. It is the truth about *myself,* and consists of an inner reality with certain outer manifestations. The manifestations can be proved and measured, but not the inner reality, or that deeper self, which gives to the outer manifestations their unity. There have been people to whom the diverse facts about the movements of my conscious or outer self and all this is real, but not the deeper truth within me, which is one. It requires no help from logic for me to realize the *Satyam,* the truth that One exists who not only comprehends all

the facts of my life, but who transcends them.

—— Rabindranath Tagore: " The Philosophical Approach to Sriniketan" incorporated in L.K. Elmhirst: *Rabindranath Tagore: Pioneer in Education*, Visva-Bharati, 1961, pp. 85-86.

The transcendence of man, as Tagore introspects in terms of social consciousness, is the inner Truth of fulfilment of whatever is best in man and society. How to eliminate the limitations of man who fails to become aware of social consciousness and social responsibilities? Where does actually lie the seeds of disintegration of human relationship? The religion of oneness of humanity is the only religion that manifests the true spirit of socialism. For such a spirit to be cultivated in right earnest Tagore probes into the causes of all our social ills and highlights that religion which is concerned with the cohesion of social consciousness. As he poignantly appeals:

> If we are engaged in disseminating the religion of strength in our country now-a-days, even then, is there no possibility of danger in that affair? Is that danger an outcome from that end whom we consider to be our enemies? Do frenzy, injustice and coersion not strike at its root in the disguise of strength? Does genuine weakness in the form of indiscipline not feign forcefulness? What is not strength but a massacre of peace appears as the most formidable one in the pursuit of strength. At present, the signs of its appearance are being visible in our country everywhere, but those amongst us who do not in fact hurst it, they, too, do not make any endeavour to keep it away by means of unpardonable rigorous discipline and repudiation. If the strength that stands for religion, would have been clearly comprehensible to

us, then we could not have for a single moment, tolerated this ukase

—— Rabindranath Tagore: "*Deshhit* "("The Wellbeing of the Country"), *Rabindra Rachanavali*, Government of West Bengal, Rabindranath Tagore Centenary Edition , 1961, Vol. XII p. 919.

[Transtaled by me.

Canvassing for a genuine urge for social consciousness necessitates a sense of social unity to be translated into reality and, for Tagore, the pulse of the society is to be felt not in isolation but in involvement both individual and social. The roots of unity are nowhere else than in the heartland of society and, for any one to be socially useful, the essential components of behavioural designs are to be renewed in terms of justice, discipline, eagerness and sincerity which are gravely lacking in the practical courses of action or involvement. As a matter of fact, the truth of man as a social being is lost in the melee of abstractions often exhibited otherwise in patterns of sham aroma and utilitarianism, affluence and avarice. A sense of mutual disbelief gradually creeps in. Since ambition mocks at social interdependence on mutual march for the ascent of man as a great social force, the consequential factors of the former rapidly and rampantly increase. The frenzied beckonings of hatred and destruction show the dismal picture of a satanic society. Whither modernity? Whither social cohesion?

For Tagore, the efflorescence of social awareness is the outcome of the inner being that fully endorsed the cause of the well-being of each and every one near and far. As a consequence, the harmony of human relationship symbolizes the spirit of global social awareness *Vasudhaiva Kutumvakam*. This harmony is the harmony of inner vision blessed not in isolation but in embracing the tiniest of all creation. It paves avenues for synchronization vision and realization. The All

Beautiful appears in the image of man as a social image of unison.

Admittedly, Tagore appeals to the social self more than mere strengthening of the soul in the island of isolation to encounter the evanascent spirit of joy and fulness of vision. As an introspective social visionary, he adroitly portrays the image of the All Beautiful in the musings of unparalleled poignance:

> Leave this chanting and singing and telling of beads! Whom dost thou worship in this lonely dark corner of a temple with doors all shut? Open thine eyes and see God is not before thee!
>
> He is there where the tiller is tilling the hard ground and where the pathmaker is breaking stones. He is with them in sun and in shower, and his garment is covered with dust. Put off thy holy mantle and even like him come down on the dusty soil!
>
> Deliverance ? Where is this deliverance to be found? Our master himself has joyfully taken upon him the bonds of creation; he is bound with us all for ever.
>
> Come out of thy meditations and leave aside thy flowers and incense! What harm is there if thy clothes become tattered and stained? Meet him and stand by him in toil and in sweat of thy brow.

—— Rabindranath Tagore: *Gitanjali (Song Offerings)* Macmillan India Limited, Macmillan Pocket Tagore Edition, 1983, No. XI. pp 6-7.

To come close to the kindred humanity is the lesson that Tagore sincerely disseminates in the education of being -- the education that comprehends the most desirable lesson of social harmony. The joy of the divine in man is indeed the joy of sociability, the joy of synchronized living in communicative and close endearment. To eliminate and destroy this social synchronization of mankind is to invite extinction of humanity. Tagore's own introspective vision reveals the truth:

The aspects of distance and nearness are both existent in the endless. It is not that the extent to which man has marred the harmonization between the near and the distant religion has become incomplete on its part, but it has become harmful. And, for this reason alone, whatever agonies are created in the world by man in the name of religion is not less than that in the pretext of worldliness. There is end of human massacre committed so far in the name of religion and is still being committed. That massacre is not merely of human life but also intelligence, kindness and love. ****But in course of all these deformations and failures, the real and everlasting entity of religion is being exposed. The reblel in man is trying to tear himself apart only to cut off all the impediments—root and branch. In the end, man has come to realize this truth: the worship of the endless is never an elimination of any component of humanity but it is the culmination of humanity in fulness.

—— Rabindranath Tagore: " Chhoto O Bodo", Santiniketan, *Rabindra - Rachanavali*, Government of West Bengal, Tagore Birth Centenary Edition, 1961, Vol. XII pp. 461-462

[Translated by me.

How far is today's education in tune with Tagore's humanistic pattern of social awareness ?

2

MASS EDUCATION AND SOCIAL CHANGE

TAGOREAN STRATEGIES

Education always caters to communication. It is a process, continual and creative, of interrelationship. As a social being, man marches ahead with the realization of a vision of unison of human creative and social excellence. The march, however, is not always smooth and easy. On the other hand, it is vitiated by narrow sentimentalism and even snobberies of so-called intellectualizm to which millions of people in our schizophrenic society are regular victims. A society in peril under such miseducation loses the charm of conjoint communicated and conscious living. It averts the avenues of sympathy and co-ordination and invites hatred and dissociation. It misses the thrilling adventure of a rapidly emerging society as it should always be and envelops itself with the dark gloom of frustration and desolation.

In fact, the role of education in creating and stimulating mass awareness is the prime need of the hour. Education alone can successfully negotiate the prevailing ills, whatsoever, of a society. It alone can take up the challenge to bring about a real, meaningful and promising revolution in the society. Today education— who denies?— toys with erudite experimentations and high promises only to end in abstractions, ambiguities and utter futility. With the apparent show of an egalitarian society, ours is a society where the education of the masses is duped in dollshouses where the ultimate objectives are neither socialization nor education but, in some form or other, institutionalization to negotiate political gains, in particular, by fair means or foul. Consequently, the vast expanse of the society, rural as well as urban, reels under uncertainties and misinformations, harrowing gloom and frustration. And what about mass education ? It is simply in a mess. Who averts the hapless lot of the people who are virtually socially ostracized in a continually camouflaged pattern of education imparted to meet special ends in view ?

To know and feel the lot of the masses not theoretically but practically by means of coming closer to them is indeed the primary and mandatory objective of education. And, for this, education should be as close to reality as possible.

In a message to the pupils read out by Tagore himself at the Classic Theatre, Calcutta on 17 *Chaitra*, 1311 Bengali era and later on published in the *Bangadarsan* in *Baisakh* next year, the following extract serves as an exemplary guideline to mass education:

> Devoid of reality, what with the mind or with the heart or even with imagination, there is the possibility of narrowness and deformity. Our patriotism proves this point. There is no connection between this welfare and the welfares of the country. The people of the coun-

try are dying of diseases, suffering from poverty and are being spoilt by noneducation and ill-education. Those who do not associate themselves with their endeavour whatsover to eliminate these ills, imagine to have achieved, by various improper imitation, the bookish patriotism of foreign literature and history. For this, even after so many years, this patriotism failed to devote ourselves to admit sacrifice. The people of the country where patriotism is not devoid of reality or not dependent on bookish imitation, are easily sacrificing their lives for the cause of the motherland. We cannot offer a little money, nor do we spare a little time for her. We do not feel any enthusiasm to know, through the spirit of enquiry, what our country actually is. Yoshida Torajiro was an eminent patriot of Japan. At the initial stage, by taking with him a little food, he gradually went on trekking the whole country on foot. Thus, by knowing the country very scrupulously, he engaged himself thereafter in teaching pupils. Towards the last stage, he had to sacrifice his life for the service of the country. The meaning of such a type of patriotism becomes revealing. When patriotism makes its foundation on the real knowledge and activities of the country, then alone it brings forth fruit like a tree that has its roots firmly stamped on the soil.

—— Rabindranath Tagore: " *Chhatrader Prati Sambhesan* " ("Address to the students"), *Siksha*, Visva-Bharati, 1973. p.23.

[Translated by me.

Like Yoshida Torajiro, the celebrated patriot of Japan, who had his initiation into the service for the society by actually associating himself closely to the social milie, Tagore also wants patriotism to be christened in the social conditions of the country from diverse dimensions. This will be a greater sacrifice, a far more intensive appeal to rouse the people of the country to be truly educated and to worthily contribute to the cause of national and global emancipatism. Learning, then, also becomes very effective and pulsating in promoting self-consciousness and self-identity with different social stratas of the country. What Tagore categorically points out through his revolutionary approach to mass education for social consciousness is that with the deep rooted urge for knowing the diverse language, religion, and culture of a society through field study as a practical approach to education for social understanding and social awareness, the learner becomes poignantly involved in opening newer avenues of social change. Indeed, the vision of a great social revolutionary cannot but be intensely correlated to the roots of the society where ordinary striving toiling masses eke out their livelihood and encompass different languages, creed and religion with a surprising note of harmony and tolerance. It is this cultivation of strength and vigour through learning and identification with the morass of the society that emancipates one from dissociation consequential to self-imprisonment in alien knowledge that gradually eats up all vitalities inherent in one as a social being. It is this cultivation of strength and vigour, again, that lifts one from the dungeon of drabness and passivity and points one towards the direction of the education of loving and being - the education of joy in unison with one and all. As an unparalleled social visionary, Tagore appeals to all concerned in mass education for social consciousness to instil our learners with the individual and group spirit of enquiry to study indigenous resources related to social cohesion. Education, then, will be truly meaningful and living, precious and pulsating. In this connection, his own elaborate and critical exposition of the role of the *Bangiya Sahitya Parishad (The Bengal Literary Association)* deserves appropriate attention:

> There is not a single state in Bengal

where, at different places, new *religious* communities are not being evolved among uneducated people. The educated people are never in the know of all these. They never consider that an enormous community of masses is set afoot unnoticed. It is not true that they are remained seated unmoved because we do not look at them in indignity. The new spirit of the new era does actually go on working within them for change. It is not possible to know the country without knowing in which way that change is going on or what form it is conceiving. I do not say that it is the ultimate aim to know the country. There is a significance to know well the actions and reactions of all human beings whatsoever and wheresoever. There is a learning in the endeavour at reading the living man directly by leaving books. As a consequence, one not only knows but also develops a spirit to know, which cannot at all be developed by reading in classes. If the pupils, with the leadership of the Association, can bring all the informatics related to the religious communities among the people of the lower classes of their own states, they would also receive the education to look at people with attention and at the same time would be able to serve the country also.

It is not that we do not read books on anthropology that is ethnology. But when we see that we do not feel the slightest form of enthusiasm to have a full-fleged account of the earthenware workers, cremation assistants, fishermen, weavers living beside us due to our bookish learning of that sort, then alone we can understand what a great superstition has grown up among ourselves about books, how great we

> consider books and how insignificant we know about him who is reflected by means of books. But if once, by leaving all abstractions, we enter into the original abode of knowledge, there would be no end to our curiosity. If our pupils engage themselves well in all-round search of all these neighbours of theirs, there is no doubt that they would receive rewards of service in service itself.

-Ibid. pp. 24-25.

[Translated by me.

Non-education or ill education that eats up the vitalities of human growth and development necessitates a positive change by means of a change of consciousness. And the roots of human progress to be solidly stamped on the ground awaits that pattern of patriotism which comes from within and not from without in either sacrifice or redemption in course of social evolution. What is the ultimate objective of social evolution? How can social awareness bring forth rebirth in mankind? How is human love born of social harmony and charity-a pointer to liberation of the soul? When does man, a new social phoenix, make the unison between dependence on the social self and that on the supreme self? Tagore, a profound thinker of social evolution, wants to assess humanity not in terms of materialism but in terms of serene spiritualism which indicates the true education for social perfection. As he poignantly elucidates:

> Then, where is our freedom amidst the world? In love. Whenever we would know that needs are not the essentials of the human society but love alone is its profound and elite shelter, then, within a moment we would be free from all shackles. Only then, we would cry out. Love, ah, what a relief. No more words, then.

> For love is an entity within myself. It is not that it compels me by giving me a fillip from outside. If love alone is the theory of the human society, then it is certainly my theory. Therefore, I have, within a moment, been promoted to the world of the freedom of joy, being emancipated from the world of necessity by dint of Love. It is as if the dream is shattered within the twinkling of eyes.
>
> This, then, is freedom. What, then? Then is dependence. As soon as love enjoys emancipation it becomes busy in fulfilling its strength in that very arena of emancipation. Then it becomes more active than before. Then, it becomes a slave to the poor, too, of the world and even serves the wicked and the down-trodden. This is the catastrophe of emancipation.

—— Rabindranath Tagore: " Emancipation in the Society" *Santiniketan, Rabindra Rachanavali,* Government of West Bengal, Calcutta, 1961, Birth Centenary edition, Vol. XII. p. 175.

[Translated by me.

As a social connoisseur of consciousness, Tagore waits for that education which will be whole-heartedly geared to the mission for emancipation of the self for the prized dependence on the supreme I, the All Enlightened. For this, an individual necessitates a greater involvement, a nobler sacrifice to social beckonings. It has its worthy dividends in the form of the self the ever disturbing irresistible little I that continually undergoes purification in the poignance of inner excellence. It has its most prized dividend in the fusion of the self and the All Beautiful, the supreme self, and this actually indicates the role of the individual as an inseparable part of the society in eliminating all confusion that serves as a forceful component in realizing the true vision of the All Beautiful in relation to man and society.

Is there any significance of the individual as an individual in being and in becoming only as an individual ? What is the role of others in the society in relation to an individual? How to be an individual as a worthly exponent of the society? How to prepare oneself for the society, and why ? All these and numerous other queries related the individual's being and becoming as a significant partner to the wellbeing of the society are vital to the true significance of man as man. Tagore characteristically elucidates all these queries from his unique approach to the genesis of mass education as follows:

> When we come within ourselves alone, then we are life; when we advance towards all, then we are living; then alone we know ourselves. When we are alone, we are none then.
>
> Our real significance is not within ourselves. That is spread over everything in this world. That is why we are seeking for that everything continually with all our intelligence and with all our hearts and with all our actions. We are continually wanting to be in unison with everything. Otherwise, we fail to have ourselves within us. The only desire of the self is to realize the self everywhere.
>
> * * * * * *
>
> Likewise, we would visualize ourselves as existent everywhere, and if this is so, we would then truly visualize ourselves. The more extensively would we know this truth of the self, the more would we receive joy. Whoever pulls himself off from within and manifests in a truer pattern, is considered to be our relative. He alone gives us joy.

> For this very reason, the only original significance within the creation of the houses, the society, the state whatsoever made by the human soul from time immemorial is that by giving up loneliness of an individual, man would realize himself in a greater sphere by means of extending his diverse strength in numerous relationships amongst the legion and the diverse and this is his real happiness. And for this it is said: *'bhumaiva sukham nalpe sukhamasti'*: vastness is happiness, no happiness is there in littleness. It is because with littleness the soul also becomes paltry.
>
> As a civilized society embraces the legion with the soul in diverse dimensions, it becomes a glory to the society. Also its significance does not entail in affluence and assemblage of advantages alone.

——Rabindranath Tagore: *Santiniketan, Rabindra Rachanavali,* Government of West Bengal, Calcutta, 1961, Birth Centenary Edition Vol. XII. p. 144.

[Translated by me.

The education of the masses necessitates such a genesis of approach as above to rise above littleness and adorn vastness. The components of social change, therefore, are those that make a desirable harmony of the wills and aspirations of the individual and the masses to bring forth social consciousness in a diverse manner. What does education actually do? What does the individual do for the real and significant advancement of the masses in the society ? How, on the other, is the society really aware of the efflorescence of individuality ? How can the evil forces of social awareness be eliminated in order to bring man closer to man and yet maintain the uniqueness of individuality? For Tagore, all these and numerous other allied queries await the desirable role of education. As true education is always an introspection with a view to associating oneself to the society to discharge one's duties to serve as best as possible, true social awareness unfolds avenues for healthy mass regeneration by means of knowledge and erudition, understanding and appreciation. For this, education makes a wider perspective for the masses for convergence side by side with divergence of multidimensional stints of experience. Tagore, of course, goes a step further in the beyonding of knowledge and experience, experiment and appreciation in mass education as a strategy for social change. He also advances in disseminating the spirit of aesthetics in mass awareness for change in social thinking. This has its two-fold purpose. The first one is to arrest the romantic veins of the individualistic and socialistic patterns of our ends in view of social change. The second is to allow and manifest the sense of restraint ably and worthily guided by the components of Truth, Beauty and Goodness to realise and appreciate worthwhile dividends of mass education for social change.

In tune with the above ends in view of mass education for social change, Tagore highlights Truth to be honoured at all costs in our approach to education formal or informal, individual or mass. For him, the approach makes no special significance as, according to him, this is the very approach that India has been nourishing and exercising from time to time. This makes education normal and natural because truth originates from the natural course of action and contemplation in which education plays the part of a booster to truth. In the other language, Truth is *tapasya*, a striving continual to what is best, worthiest and most natural in a natural atmosphere. Mass education, therefore, must embrace this natural course of learning in a society.

In this connection, Tagore's own viewpoints on national education are very significant. As he observes:

> It would be an utter mistake in our approach to understanding national education as it is realised by Europe. The process of aggravating the prestige of our own nation by delimiting through special customs and folk-dealings of our nation cannot by any means be considered national education by me.
>
> Our nationalism is that we do not worship nationalism to be the ultimate aim of each one of us. *Bhumaiva sukham, nalpe sukhamasti, bhumateva vijijnasitavyah* (Vastness is happiness, no happiness is derived by means of littleness, vastness should be endeared as one's own self): this, then, is the motto of our nationalism.

—— Rabindranath Tagore: "Tapovan", *Siksha*, Visva-Bharati, 1973. pp. 97-98.

[Translated by me.

Mass education for social awareness, indeed, awaits a newer approach to highlight dissemination of Truth. It is a quest eternal, unending, unique. It is a quest, again, that calls forth mass awakening of consciousness to rise above the polluting and derogatory current of passivity and abstraction. It is an infinite endeavour to enrich individuality for the common good of the society. It is an education where every individual is never lost in the melee' of the masses but is *reenlivened* to foster the spirit of individual creative and critical power of thinking. This is a natural process and this never comes or poses as a threat to mass unity. What type of mass education for social awareness is possible when the masses are in a mess due to its being a victim to a generalised and streamlined course of action? Why mass education when education loses mobility or dynamism as it is clearly evident in today's exhibitionism in the name of mass education to bring about social awareness? Tagore is very critical of such a strategy for launching mass education that misses the essential aims and objectives of social regeneration. He, therefore, never compromises with sociability or social awareness in course of educating the masses that has proneness to kill the soul of education by means of stifling individual efflorescence in creative and aesthetic consciousness. The art of being a social human being in the midst of a multi-dimensional society necessitates cultivation of Truth, Beauty and Goodness as the ultimate aim of every action or exposure and this is more often than not dwarfed, ignored or belittled in the romantic spree in the name of mass education or social education even now as it was evident in a colonialistic society of ours in the Tagorean period. Moreover, a certain sense of passivity often aggravates an individual's approach to be educated through self-endeavour and self-enrichment, where mass education either remains silent or pulls forth streamlined dynamism that deranges finer feelings and softer delicacies of life. Life lost in bare living and not enriched in emancipation of the little self by means of exercise of individuality is no life at all but paradoxically 'lovely remains of death'.

As a practical social thinker, Rabindranath always upholds individuality above social snobberies that eat up vitalities of introducing mass education. The 'education of sympathy, the highest education as he categorically asserts, warns individuality against erosion of the fundamental principle of mass education that imparts the lesson of kinship with all around us and not only with human beings. In his own words,

> The highest education is that which does not merely give us information but makes our life in harmony with all existence.

—— Rabindranath Tagore: "My School", *Personality*, p.116

Mass education for an educated mind that cares for an all embracing social enrichment in harmony and not for miseducation in marooned awareness ably nourished and nurtured in informatics brings about a routinized pattern of social change that is more often putted up in statistical jargons than on mass awakening of good sense and sensibilities.

Leaving aside the muse of rhythm derived through the creative world of poetry. Tagore has in his heart of hearts the dream of mass education for social change. He has nurtured this dream right from his boyhood. He always thinks of translating that dream into 'practice' as he frankly states in *Sanivarer Chithi*, a journal of literary criticism, in its *Vaishakh* issue of 1347 B.S. In his Pabna Address in 1908 , he also refers to his endeavour at experimentations of his socio-educational thoughts that are deeply enriched with the newer dimensions of social regeneration.

What Tagore actually wanted for reawakening of social awareness by means of mass education is to reenkindle the spirit of nationalism without yielding to the yoke of foreign ideas, foreign thoughts and foreign sentiments or to poverty that has nothing to do with upholding dignity which rests on true education. He, therefore, advocates a radical approach to social consciousness that allows no compromise with either poverty or independence but wins over untoward forces through cultivation of sympathy, education and spiritualism which enriches develpment of manifold traits of personality. In elucidating the role of a true *brahmin*, the disseminator of erudition for social and all-round awareness for fulness of man, Tagore make a very significant analyses:

> Our modern *brahmins* took recourse to the profession of receiving honour *sans* remuneration. As a consequence, their honour has gradually become oral in our society. This is not all. To bring about slothness in the dignified work to which the *brahmins* were appointed,

the cohesion in society is also being splittered day by day.

If the society is to be safeguarded in the eastern way, if drastic change of this age-old big society is neither possible nor desirable by means of the European process, then there is an urgent necessity of this real *brahmin* community. They would be poor as well as scholars and devoted to religion. They would be like an ideal and refuge of the ashramic spirit from diverse avenues as well as *gurus* or preceptors.

There is no disgrace in dependence or poverty to that society where a group of people knows how to ignore the affluent, hates luxuries, whose manners are pure, devotion to religion firm and who are engaged in selfless pursuit or dissemination of knowledge. A society that makes one duly honourable is alone honoured by one in return.

—— Rabindranath Tagore: *Brahman Rabindra Rachanavali,* Government of West Bengal, Calcutta. Birth Centenary Edition, 1961. Vol. XII, p. 1030

[Translated by me.

To place man in the society on the platform of dignity by means of devotion to knowledge and the true spirit of self-sacrifice is the keynote of Rabindranath Tagore's mass education. It is that education which inculcates the spirit of sympathy and service to mankind in the same spirit of service to the Almighty. The approach is always a laborious one but it must be supported by the true spirit of education that fosters an ideal living condition in the society that enkindles the light of manhood in man.

Deeply concerned with the inherent spirit of man as a social being, Tagore emphasizes on a disciplined mind of every individual in the society. The posterity of a country is, as he firmly believes, always dependent on how her people are alive to the spirit of social consciousness by means of efflorescence of mass education. This necessitates a sense of inner dynamic appeal to which every one responds with an educated and disciplined mind. Tagore makes a characteristic appeal time and again to eliminate this sense of passivity that greatly affects social and living cohesion. As he elucidates:

> In spite of exposing the image of greatness of our country the constraint in accepting that lies in weakness of our power. We were devoid of a strong and stable possession but our pride was on the increase. A time was there in you when we amassed all the perversions of our society and religion owing to our ritualities and were enclosed within those enclosures. Now it is due to pride alone that we consider it a symptom of strength by admitting all the perversions forcibly. We won't sweep the room, nor would we throw any garbage outside, everything as existent anywhere we would endear and consider it a principle of cooperation by injudiciously safeguarding the gems and jewels along with the dust-such, then, is the plight of affairs that have taken place amongst us. It is, indeed, ignorance. It is passivity that equally valuates everything as existent anywhere and safeguards them. To it, good and evil, error and truth are one and the same.

—— Rabindranath Tagore: "*Khrista*" ("The Christ"), *Rabindra-Rachanavali*, Government of West Bengal, Calcutta, Birth Centenary, Edition, 1961. Vol. XI, p. 504.

[Translated by me.

What prompts Tagore in launching social regeneration by means of mass education is to enforce vitality and eliminate passivity in man. It is to arouse the urgent need for self-awakening through education of the self that has poignance of promise to be truly social and humanistic. It is education and education alone as he strongly asserts that eliminates ignorance just as light drives away darkness. In his essay entitled *Sikshar Vahan*, Tagore highlights the importance of dissemination of education among the masses by means of proper and widespread use of the mother tongue only to make the light of knowledge and advancement of learning easy and simple for the masses in our society. This will really allow a festival of mutual understanding and appreciation of man as man mingling in the social idealism of sympathy and co-operation, mutual love and devotion. Hence, education for social excellence.

Mass education, therefore, is as Rabindranath Tagore categorically asserts, the *sin qua non* of social regeneration. The first strategy that he applies for such social regeneration is the introduction of the mother-tongue as the most effective means of accelerating social awareness, social harmony and social understanding. He painfully unfolds the attitudes of the so-called educated people who still nurture the much harmful downward filtration theory of education by Lord Curzon who was more interested in education for the elite few than in mass education. He also appeals to the social heritage of mankind which acts as a guiding force in stimulating mass education. The absence of the true and effective medium of education by means of fostering and honouring the mother-tongue on the one hand and channelising the pulsating social vision of mass awareness not by political acrobatics but through devotion to mass education with all seriousness which happily enjoyed holidays in the name of haphazard and aimless struggle for independence with practically no struggle for education to cater to mass social transformation that even now goes abegging in the whirlwind of faulty and society-shy plans and programmes of mass education necessitates a rethinking, restructuring and re-evaluating of education for mass consciousness and social change in the light of the Tagorean viewpoints that are still relevant and significant:

> The main point is: modern education has not got its medium: its movements have not been free. Universal education has by now been accepted in every civilised country. Whatever might be the reason, this was not in vogue in our country. Mahatma Gokhale fought for this. I have heard that he has faced maximum constraints from Bengal. In the sphere of good sense there is a peenliar wind of epidemic blowing on all of a sudden in Bengal from every direction at present.
>
> We have decided that in our movements in the world we would go backward, only in our flight towards national pursuit we would fly forward. Our wings would grow just opposite to our legs.
>
> Nowhere was there any response to that universal education which would act as a sustenance to the roots of higher education in the country. Moreover, another symptom has cropped up. The area of our limited higher education has been further squeezed by increasing the furniture on the one hand and lessening the space on the other. Let there be want of pupils but no lack of equipments: our keen attention is towards that direction.
>
> * * * * * *
>
> I admit that for mankind a dish is as important as food, but when it is not being available for the poor, there is definitely a necessity for a bit contral over the dish. When I

> would visualize that there are centres for dissemination of food of learning all over India, then the day would come when we would demand golden dish from the goddess of food, *annapurna.* If our mode of living is like the poor but the external pomp of our education is like the rich, then it would be like making a money bag by bungling with the money.

—— Rabindranath Tagore: "*Sikshar Vahan*", *Siksha,* Visva-Bharati 1973 pp.143-144

[Translated by me.

What Tagore actually *wants* for dissemination of mass education is to inculcate the spirit of social sobriety which would eliminate the appalling difference between the rich and the poor, the advantaged and the disadvantaged, the privileged and the deprived, the educated and the illiterate in the vast social panorama of mankind in our country. He, therefore, strongly, suggests for austerity in our approach to mass education for social consciousness and upholds the examples of illustrious persons of our country who have come of very poor families of our society but who have always set priceless examples in mingling with the haves and have-nots of the society in the same platform, shared their weals and woes, achievements and failures in organising and participating in the activities of the one big Social Family of our nation and contributed very effectively towards better social emancipation of man as man. What is essentially required in case of mass education is not affluence but sincerity of purpose in our educational strategies and endeavour.

The education of being simple and sobre is the highest education that cannot, as Tagore strongly advocates, but be an indispensable strategy of mass education for advancement of social awareness. This alone indicates our true identity, the identity of a strong nation with socially conscious persons already prepared to devote themselves to the cause of one another. What type of simplicity as a characteristic feature of mass education does Rabindranath suggest? What components are of utmost importance that would bring forth the sense of togetherness in academic endeavour so that the whole society becomes aware, living, pulsating, responsive, critical and creative to prove itself active and dynamic to stand up as one indivisible unit of unity and strength? In the light of fulness of education for fulness of the social man, he poignantly delves deep into the worth and progress of humanism as follows:

> I never consider poverty to be great. That is ephemeral. But austerity is more valuable than the consuming materials of the affluent. That is real. I am speaking of that austerity which represents an idea of fulness and not merely absence of affluence. When there would be an awakening of that idea, then, within the twinkling of our eyes, much darkness of the mist of materialism would disappear from the firmament of civilization. As there is the absence of that idea, the things that are of utmost importance to every man are becoming costly and beyond dependence. Music, food, tourism, entertainment, education, administration, law and order all are very complicated in a civilized country, all have encroached upon a vast room both inside and outside man. Much of this burden is redundant. The strength of an individual is, of course, revealed in the carrying out of this massive burden, but it does not spell out his abilities. For this reason the God, who is looking at modern civilization externally is visualizing it like a demon, an unskilled swimmer's attempt to swim. The water sprinkled out of his strokes of legs and hands is whirling and foaming, he even does not know that there is no real

> need for his so much desperation. The difficulty is: the demon is of firm conviction that there is a special value of kicking hands and legs with a terrific speed. When there will be an awakening of simple truth of fulness in the heart, then, from the walls of the western drawing room, the Japanese fan, the Chinese utensils, the horns of the deer, the skin of the tiger—the diverse meaninglessness spread throughout its corners—would vanish like evil visions. From the hats of maidens, dead birds, feathers, artificial flowers, leaves and heaps of garbages would drop down: their over dealings with dresses and decorations would find their place in the archeology of barbarism. The five or ten storeyed buildings standing with their fists raising towards the sky would bend their heads in shame. What with education or with work or with consumerism, to be christened with the ideal of simplicity would be considered by them the true identity of strength and the inherent nature of man will seize the kingdom of the slaves of external one and keep them seated at its legs.
>
> —*Ibid.* pp. 145-146
>
> [Translated by me.

The education of simplicity born out of loading a simple, harmonious and dedicated life in the society is the *sine qua non* of mass education for social excellence. It is this excellence for which Rabindranath intends to encourage knowing oneself in being simple, revealing oneself in being simple, activating oneself towards the welfare of others in being simple and dedicating oneself to the cause of greater social cohesion. Not apeing western socialism already doled out in materialism and abstraction, utilitarianism and afflu ence, but striving unendingly in the pursuit of social excellence by means of fostering mass education for all round development of personality is the fundamental objective of education that Tagore gives priority in promoting social awareness in our country. Who ignores that his vision of mass education for social consciousness badly awaits poignant rethinking right now?

It is interesting to note in this connection that Tagore makes education rather than achievement of national independence more important to bring about social change. The social values cannot be properly achieved in the life of an individual unless these are transferred through the process of education that leads to perfection of man. Inculcation of good ideals in the society is of prime importance to understand social values and for this education is the only means to understand the real worth of achievement of independence. Good education for every child in the society, therefore, follows good ideals in the society. In his own categorical statement Tagore clarifies the point as follows:

> If the values be perverted, no sort or amount of formal education can save the child from their destructive effect. Good education of children is not possible unless good ideals govern the society.

Raindranath Tagore: "Message to the New Education Fellowship Conference at Calcutta", *Visva-Bharati News* January 1938

When Tagore speaks of universal education, it encompasses education for all in the society and not a certain section — coterieprone of self-conscious and self-interested. Again, it broadens its scope to wider dimensions of society not because the masses should merely undergo education for the sake of education geared to ban livelihood but education that teaches everyone how to be a worthy contributor to the all round welfare of the society - intellectual, moral, aesthetic, spiritual, religious, economic and so on. With this categorical and specific unit of universal education to bring about mass awareness Tagore studies the primary hurdles of social consciousness and emergence of 'men, from 'man'. Then, and then only, education can be effectively linked to bring about desirable social change. Then, and then only, education will encourage the innovative spirit in every learner young and old, and become truly 'national' in character. Tagore's invaluable suggestions in this connection are still relevant:

> Certainly, the sphere of learning in our country would, by any means, be freed from the encagement of walls. By frittering our endeavour through external strategies like political movement and the like we are not having any special outcome. We will have to shoulder the responsibility of imparting education independently to our countrymen amongst ourselves by channelizing our strength and effort towards the avenue of success. This alone is the most fundamental duty of those who want to sacrifice themselves for the sake of the country. When we will be able to mobilize the current of education in our country in course of manifold experimentations by different teachers, only then education will turn out to be a natural outcome of our country. Only then we will come across true teachers at different places from time to time. Only then, generations of teachers would naturally emerge in spontaneity. We cannnot innovate a special method of education by labelling it 'national'. We can name that education as 'national' which is being directed by diverse endeavour of different people of our own nation. Whether by rule indigenous or foreign, when a particular method of education

> wants to encompass the whole country with a fixed ideal then I would not certify it as 'national', it is communal, and so it is dangerous for the nation.

—— Rabindranath Tagore: "Sikshavidhi", *Siksha*, Visva-Bharati 1973. p. 128

[Translated by me.

To eliminate 'communal' education in the name of 'national' education, Tagore makes the windows of education wide open in his own educational experimentations at Sriniketan. His own school, Siksha-Satra, is the altar of learning the fundamental lessons of mass consciousness for the young and vibrant learners of nearby villages, who learn the lessons of self-help and sympathy, co-operation and tolerance and above all, the worth of freedom and creativity in a conjoint society. What type of teachers are necessary to impart such type of education? What should be their primary responsibilities to generate a warmth of learning by leading a true social life side by side with national and global life ? What, again, should be their method of education for awakening of social awareness amongst learners? Tagore's view points on the same deserve rethinking in right earnest:

> We learnt a great truth about education. We knew that man can learn from man alone just as a reservoir is filled only with water, a flame is enkindled only by another flame, and a life is ignited only by another life. As soon as a man is clipped, he ceases to be a man; he, then, turns out to be an important commodity of the office or mills and factories. Just then he wants to be a teacher instead of being a man. Just then he faiis to impart life and, on the other hand, imparts lessons only. Amid relationship of total kinship between the teacher and the disciple,

the activities in education can go on like the stream of blood of a vibrant body. This is due to the fact that the real responsibility of rearing and educating children lies on parents. But as they have not that ability and advantage, the assitance of other appropriate persons becomes mandatory.

Under such circumstances, a teacher cannot but be parents. We cannot purchase the best thing of life by money, nor can we accept it partially, we can assimilate it by means of love, affection and devotion only. That is the enzyme of the digestive organ of humanity, that alone can unite living commodities with life. At present, in the education of our country, the life of that type of teacher has become very necessary. There is nothing more dangerous than lifeless education in childhood. It extracts more than what it offers the mind by grinding. In the social system of our country we are seeking that teacher who would bring forth dynamism in our life. We are seeking that teacher in our system of education, who would eliminate all constraints that stand in the way of the course of movements of our mind. From every direction, we want man by any means howsoever. Instead, no physician can save us by making us gobble up the pill of procedures.

— Ibid pp. 128-129.

What, then, is essentially required in launching mass education for emergence of social awareness is to fully equip the organisational avenues of education with a band of devoted and sincere teachers who are always prepared to impart living education the education that allows the learner to manifest the 'men' in the best possible avenues of excellence.

The finer sensibilities of life such as love, fellow-feeling, tolerance etc. await a social and humane touch in the most practical fashion and for this, the sense of true neighbourliness should be nurtured through the education of social values and social aesthetics. Tagore makes a significant point of departure from other social thinkers and organisers in highlighting education as a means of inner awareness that ultimately leads to practice in poignance of the great Upanishadic saying: *bhumaiva sukham nalpe sukhamasti.* Happiness, indeed, is the outcome of embracing vastness by eliminating every aspect of littleness in man. The teacher who is himself an integral part of the society understands best the loopholes of social consciousness. It is he who can best enable the learners right from the beginning of education to identify the harmful seeds of social disharmony and to strengthen them to innovate new avenues of better and more effective social awareness.

The true concept of nationhood as Tagore believes and elucidates in his many writings is also based on how to be globally conscious as a true social being. The education geared to this end in view is what makes every man a global man in the global society. Tagore, of course, goes a step further in highlighting education for social transcendence and crystallizes the vision of the social man by means of embracing tradition and culture ancient and modern. The essence of social conciousness thus enjoys a favourable environment of efflorescence in every human being in the society. The education that he wants to be disseminated in the society is, therefore, the education to uphold the past glory and culture of a country to forge ahead towards the future for better social emancipation. In this connection, his own elucidation of the true concept of 'nation' deserves rethinking:

> Nation is a living existent, a mental matter. Two things have composed the inner nature of this matter. Those two things are, in fact, the same. Of these, one is existent in the

past, the other at present. One is the old treasure of reminiscence of one and all, the other a mutual agreement, a desire to live together-a desire to appropriately safeguard the transfer of undivided inheritance. Man does not readily build himself by single handed endeavour. In the same way, the nation also continues to be manifested in course of endeavour of the long past time, renouncement of the self, and sincerity. We have been, to a great extent, made by our incestors. The origin of the fundamentals of the national idea lies in heroism, greatness and achievements of the past. The same glory of the masses of the past and the same desire of the masses at present, to accomplish a great work together in the past and the resolution to again accomplish that type of work together-this alone is the source point of framing a community of masses. Our love will be forceful to the extent of our agreement of renunciation and tolerance of sufferings. We love that house which we have built with our own hands and will deliver it to the future generation. In the song of ancient sparta there is a saying: 'We are what you were, we would be what you are'. This very simple statement is the national ballad of all countries.

—— Rabindranath Tagore: *Nation Kee"* ('What is a Nation'), *"Atmasakti O Samuha", Rabindra-Rachanavali,* Government of West Bengal, Calcutta. Tagore Birth Centenary Edition. 1961. Vol. XII, p. 677.

[Translated by me.

To safeguard the treasure of undivided and endless inheritance by means of transcendence of tradition and culture is the *sine qua non* of Tagore's views on mass education for social consciousness. It is with this end in view that he wants everyone to find out joy out of sorrow, happiness out of sufferings, mutual dependence out of diversities, tolerance out of differences, nearness out of distance. It is with this end in view, again, that he urges for embracing sorrow together, sharing joy together, craving for aspiration together. The lesson of the past is to embrace sorrow together, to share mutual responsibilities in the ascent of man as a true social being. Only then the spirit of nationalism emerges in true perspectives of social awareness.

The swansong of socialism as Tagore visualizes, awaits this enrichment of social education through mass awakenings of thought and action, creativity and devotion. For this, he advocates differences in social aims and objectives as healthy signs for promotion of individuality. Individual freedom of thought and action is the only prerogative for effective mass education that allows spontaneity and dynamism. This freedom is the most precious possession of every society, which ultimately contributes abundantly to the efflorescence of global development of mankind. As a matter of fact, it is the pioneering vision of Tagore as a social thinker that has unfolded the appalling damage done to humanity by dwarfing the inherent possibilities of an individual to prove his worth as an inseparable social being in harmonizing society with the spirit of sincerity and devotion to highlight the excellence of global humanity. For him, the concept of nation as has been envisaged in the western world makes a significant departure in being a major force for social consciousness. But in our country the idea of social emancipation primarily encompasses the society in and around ourselves. And so, when we are erroneously triggered off with the spirit of nationalism in the western pattern, our society misses much of the desired aims and objectives as evident in our failures to rejuvenate the masses to rise up as one man in the society. A dwarfed individual--dwarfed in thought, action and resolution--hardly shoulders any social responsibilities either in educating himself or others in the society. He remains alien from the masses and whatever social transformation might take place he hardly responds as desired. Added to these is the erosion of social values that teach good behaviour and honesty, renunciation and tolerance, purity and poignance of thought and action that are the invaluable contributions of our ancient society. Tagore wants to revive that essence of mass education in our society by means of which there might be a resurgence of social consciousness in idealising and actualising the great ideals of our ancient society. Let our entire programme of mass education for social awareness be vibrant with the refreshing spirit of great ideas and activities of the past. Let the spirit of dynamism of the ancient societies of India be reenlivened with the realization of inherent strength and vigour. Let there be a conscious, pulsating heart in the society--a heart that embraces all men in the society not with the force of destruction but with the spirit of all-round development of the society.

A society in which everyone cares for the well-being of others receives the best fruits of education through mass awareness. Tagore wants to imbibe that spirit of social regeneration by means of mass education. Such type of education alone can bring about a sense of curiosity among all sections of people in the society to arouse the sense of goodness in everyone's heart. Let every member of the society be inspired with that outcome of education in which food, health, all round welfare--all become an integrated and spontaneous affair in the day to day activities. This is nothing new in the Indian society that cherishes a rich tradition and culture ably and worthily guided by mass education in the society. To glorify the sacred ideals of love and co-operation, hospitality and tolerance has turned out to be an inseparable and continuous part of the education of the masses in the Indian society. The education of becoming is thus purified in the education of being which stands out to be the true education of the masses in the society. Tagore wants to revive this classical spirit of education in ancient India that stimulates man to become 'men' in the society and glorifies the vision of man as an unparalleled social being. He wants to bring forth again that spirit of Indian education that makes socialization of mankind a natural and spontaneous affair. The education that every member of the society should receive is the education of devotion and sacrifice--the education of goodness and generosity as well--that unites all sections of people in the society with the vision of oneness of man.

It is interesting to note how Tagore again and again emphasizes on the importance of indigenous education that is rooted to our native soil and discourages alien education disseminating alien tradition and culture. It is also interesting to note that he first directs the attention of all concerned with freedom of the country and mass education in the society how education of the masses has been vitiated by text-books dealing with foreign environment, culture and tradition.*

*In his doctoral thesis, Dr. H.B. Mukherjee makes a very illuminating analysis on this point as follows :

> 'Tagore many a time stressed the point that an education system of a country should be rooted in the native soil and should draw inspiration from the genius and tradition of the land with regard to its aim, content, method and organization. The atmosphere and activities of the education institutions should reflect the cultural heritage of the nation as also the changing thoughts of its people in relation to the changing conditions and needs of the time. Any blind invitation either of any foreign cultural pattern or even of one's own deat past, however, will destroy the dynamic character of [the] education and will impart to it an artificiality and unreality which will take away its vital force and effectiveness. That is why Tagore repeatedly criticized the educational pattern introduced in India under the

> British rule for being alien in character in every respect. The snow-balls, Charlies and Katies featuring in the English text-books for Indian children, the emphasis on learning a foreign language both as a subject and as the medium of instruction, the class system of teaching as in Eurpoean schools and colleges, the general pattern of educational organization under official control, the study of the western sciences like Politics, Economics, European History and Western Philosophy, and the thoughtless adoption of western ideas and ideologies through those studies and through the social atmosphere prevailing in fashionable and official circles--all these were entirely foreign to the traditional culture and values of the Indian people. Consequently, the educational system failed to take root in the country at large, while it created a conflict of ideologies among a certain section of people who were brought up in it, Tagore brought out this point in vivid and forceful language in his very first educational writing, *Sikshar Her-pher*, and never tired to repeating it whenever the occasion demanded it in his subsequent writings.

—H. B. Mukherjee: *Education for Fulness*, Asia Publishing House, Bombay. 1962. pp. 303-304.

A society thus oriented in foreign culture, foreign tradition and artificial environment makes little headway to social development and human consciousness. Tagore also harps on indigenous education with a view to allowing importance to social needs and responsibilities that make everyone aware of being habituated in self-activity, self-dependence and self development rather than being aped in arbitrary mechanization, automation and abstraction and passivity.

This is, indeed, heartening as it makes true socialization through education a reality in the best possible manner. Moreover, this adherence to indigenous education to bring about desirable social awareness is always natural and spontaneous and therefore, lively and vigorous. This is the only way of restoration of identity as a nation as well as a society. This is the only way, again, to foster the spirit of national culture, tradition and heritage that enriches individuality and nationalism. As an educationist Mahatma Gandhi also follows the same approach to mass education for ideal socialization and warns against the pitfalls of education that denies children to welcome indigenous wonderland of education for social consciousness. In his invaluable words:

> Almost from the commencement the text-books deal not with things the boys and the girls have always to deal within their homes, but things to which they are perfect strangers. *** The higher he goes, the farther removed he is from his home, so that at the end of his education he becomes estranged from his surroundings. *** His education is calculated to wean him from his traditional culture. And if the mass of educated youths are not entirely denationalized, it is because the ancient culture is too deeply embedded in them to be altogether uprooted even by our education averse to its growth.

——M.K. Gandhi: *Young India,* September 1, 1921.

What makes Tagore a unique contributor to mass education for social awareness is his approach to the fact that education to be significant and meaningful must be a continual striving process of emancipation of mankind. In other words, it is he who for the first time emphasizes on mass education which is a means to an end and never an end in itself. He denounces that type of endeavour at mass education for social awareness which is temporal, emotional and aimed at negotiating immediate satisfaction and fulfilment. Education is, as he firmly believes, never doling out sermons or the transitory aroma of satisfaction to the hapless masses who are more often *camouflaged* in sermonization than directed towards a persuasive endeavour of learning more and more to become complete and worthy citizens.

It would not be inappropriate to note in this connection that Tagore has time and again expressed his strong resentment against compartmentalized education -- a type of education, alas, even now prevalent among some sections of people in our society -- that cares for education of the privileged few and never for all. He does not approve of the Wardha scheme of education because that also caters to the enlightened few of the society. He makes the avenue of mass education wide open so that the whole of the human society be benefited by the light of education that reaches everywhere and does not betray a single person in the society. It is the ultimate end in view of education that ensures fullness of man from every area of efflorescence. Mass education is never allowed to crush in a mess of education where the appalling differences between the poor and the rich are further allowed to thrive in littleness of mind and outlook.

For a better orientation of education even at the higher levels like colleges and universities and other seats of higher learning Tagore prescribes for a renewal vision of advancement of learning in the true sense of the term by means of incorporating the rich fruits of experience gathered from our famous Indian universities of Nalanda, Taxila and so on. To make such a linkage between the modern and the ancient altars of education is to ensure a thriving and continual current of knowledge and erudition that signifies the healthy spirit of dynamism among all sections of people in the society irrespective of caste, creed, religion etc. A society thus synchronized with the bond of pursuit of learning makes mass education truly significant and meaningful as it becomes an indivisible and contributing part of education at all levels of pursuit of learning and advancement. Moreover, the little points of differences whatsoever between man and man at all levels of the society are eliminated as best as possible. The urge for mutual understanding and appreciation that leads to progress of the society becomes more thriving and pulsating as the masses never feel any sense of isolation in their common endeavour at social development.

How to bring forth the best of common endeavour for mass education in the society in order to create a healthy and natural environment of all-pervading consciousness? How to disseminate the spirit of unity, co-operation, sympathy and goodness in the society by means of education for the masses? What should be the most ideal and desirable strategies of ensuring sound and effective mass education for social awareness? Tagore makes an introspective, scientific, spontaneous and natural approach to negotiate all the askances as above. He wants everyone in the society to grow within to ensure real growth of the society He demands, and rightly so, that inner vision of man to be rekindled with better effulgence to develop within for the genuine development that every society earnestly craves for in order to leave a lasting impression of man as an incomparable social being.

To leave this lasting impression of man as a social being is as Tagore strongly advocates, the prime need for education to bring about social awareness. What he earnestly deserves as the outcome of education is to be assured of the fact that to unfold oneself continually and ceaselessly for the welfare of the society is to be truly educated. And, for this, the purpose of education would be to penetrate into the core of the society, feel its pulse and all accordingly. Then, and then only, education would keep pace with the progress of mankind playing multidimensional role in the society. The heart of the society, indeed, awaits a deeper and more sincere involvement of every man and woman in the society to build and rebuild it in accordance with the greatest vision of mankind as a social being. So when Tagore speaks of the role of education to bring about worthwhile social consciousness, he emphasizes on dynamism and development he wants everyone in the society to rededicate himself in order to maintain a certain sense of synchronization between tradition and modernity that proves the excellence of a glorified society.While making an introspective analysis of the Indian society nearly ninety years ago, he characteristically spells out this points as follows:

> The change of life is development, the change of death, a reaction. In our society, too, changes are quickly taking place, but as there is an absence of conscious heart in the society, that change is verging towards reaction and analysis. None is being able to arrest it.
>
> A new situation, new education, commotion with a new nation— these are undeniable. If we want to go on as if these are not existent, as if we push ourselves back towards three thousand years ago, then the conditions of those three thousand years would not be of any assistance to us and the flood of change now would float us away. If we do not admit the present in the plea of ancestry, the ancestors would not respond. Our ancestors are earnestly appealing to us by saying, 'save our achievements by making a treaty with the present, do not allow it to be utterly destroyed by blindly following it. Make a unison between one period and the other consciously safeguarding our chord of thinking. Otherwise, the chord will by itself be distorted'.
>
> What would have to be done ? Everyone in the country would sacrifice his own interest for the interest of the country. When the

Hindu society was alive, then the limbs and arteries of the society would consider the interest of the whole body of the society to be its only interest. The king was the very part of the society: the assignment of social security and organization was due to him. The Brahmins were engaged in glorifying and eternalizing the pure ideals of social religion in the society. Their meditation and erudition, devotion to education -- all were the property of the society. As the resident is the architect of the society, every *ashram* residence was treated so glorious. To enrich that residence by means of wisdom, religion, idea and action, diverse forces of the society would earnestly act in different directions. The rules and functions of those days were not meaningless in the backdrop of those times.

Now those rules are there, but that consciousness remains absent. There is not that endeavour in its limbs and arteries, keeping an eye to the well-being of the society. If we reestablish that eternally alive idea of goodness of our ancestors in our hearts as our living component and apply that in every sphere of our society, then we will be able to attain the vast Hindu civilization. It is our own duty to educate the society and provide it with health, food, wealth and money. Therein lies our goodness. Not to visualize it as a business but it is the only accomplishment not to hope *sans* virtue and goodness in exchange for that. That is union of action with the Supreme. To continually recall that is Hinduism. Instead of placing the ideal of the self at the centre of the human society, to observe it in the midst of the Brahma is in Hinduism. As a consequence, the idea of

> goodness towards all, from the beast to every human being, is diverged and to renunciate the self with constant practice becomes as easy as breathing. To tie everyone of the society from top to bottom with a large selfless string of goodness -- this alone is the bigger endeavour than all other efforts of ours. With this string of unity, the unison of religion should be made between the present and the past, between one and the other of the Hindu community. This is the only way for us to attain humanity.

——Rabindranath Tagore:"Bharatvarsiyas Samaj" ("The Indian Society"), *Rabindra-Rachanavali,* Government of West Bengal, Calcutta. Tagore Birth Centenary Edition. 1961. Vol. XII. pp. 682-683.

[Translated by me.

What Tagore wants to bring about by means of a certain radical chage in social outlook is to revive the sense of purity and poignance in our approach in social awareness. This necessitates the education of being side by side with the education of becoming. And, for this our best guide is the serene ancient Indian education for social consciousness for conjoint, communicated, selfless, pure and perfect living. This type of education allows a happy blending of thoughts and ideas among people of all sections of the society in the most natural, undeterred and spontaneous manner, and the sense of mutual goodness and co-operation controls the whole society against all odds and strains, ukases and constraints. As a consequence, there is a harmony of social opinions and standards in all possible diversities and dimensions, and at the root of all these, the 'man' in man grows undisturbed. When Tagore looks back towards our rich heritage and tradition, he not only ensures modernity in our approach to education for mass awareness but also ensures radicalism in thought and action, promise and perfection.

That is why he goes so far as to compel everone in the society, specially the enlightened ones, to earnestly shoulder social responsibilities of imparting education, making everyone aware of health and hygiene, economy and affluence and, above all, inspiring to be self-supporting and self-esteemed in every sphere of life. This is, indeed, a new vision of mass education for social consciousness -- a vision that allows humanity to be enriched with the spirit of social transcendence. Like a social iconoclast, Rabindranath plunges into the oddities of social prejudices writ large in our ancient social thoughts and principles of life, and radically makes adventurous inroads to find out the truth of life that stands for true socialism. As a matter of fact, he shatters age-old orthodox social customs and prejudices and unfolds truth that marks the victory of education to bring about desirable mass consciousness. He strongly vindicates those persons who glorify the past unduly and indiscriminatingly and even support evils or ills as if there are of Indian origin. He characteristically portrays these people suffering from vainglory as follows :

> Their indiscriminate reverence is for the actual, not the eternal. The habits and customs of our decadence, which have set up barriers between us and the world, splitting us into mutually exclusive sections, making us weak and bowing our heads in shame at every turn of our later history -- these are the idols of their special worship which they endow with endless virtues of their own imagining. They consider it to be their sacred mission to retain it in perpetuity the waste matter sloughed off by age, as the true insignia of our Hindu civilization; to extol the gleam of the will-o-the -wisp, born of the noxious miasma of decay, as more time-hallowed than the light of sun, moon and stars.

Quoted from *Rabindranath Nath Tagore : Poet and Dramatist* by Edward Thompson, Radhi-India Edition, Calcutta, 1979, P. 282.

Towards the waning years of his life, Rabindranath was deeply shattered with the pollution of social ignorance and instability that loomed large in the whole of the Indian society. Superstitions of peculiar forms and magnitudes, indeed, overpowered the-then Indian society where the finer aspects of humanity among the masses enjoyed unusual slumber in the darkness of mis-education. The soul of the society bereft of synchornization vehemently suffered from passivity and abstraction. Being deeply pained at heart at the triumph of utilitarianism, materialism, cowardice, and peevish mentality of a duped society, he even welcomed atheism to replace so-called religion that had eaten up the vitalities of the masses in the society.* Let there be a fresh approach to society from the educational points of view so that the masses might be reawakened with the spirit of reviving old values in our social systems and trends of life that amply contributed to social unity and cohesion, exchange of ideas and appreciation. Let there be a fresh approach to society to shoulder the responsibilities that enlighten every member of the society to understand appreciate the inner heart of the society. For this, we badly need, as Tagore strongly urges, revival of our socio-

*Edward Thompson makes a thrilling analysis of the mind of Tagore in this context

> Two years before he died, he told an English visitor that he would welcome even a wave of atheism over India, for it would act like a forest fire that sweeps away dead stuff and rubbish. When I was last in India, in October 1939, after the outbreak of war, he said, and only half in jest, that he was sorry he would not live to see the Soviet Union conquer India, for it was the only Power which would drop a bomb impartially on those two symbolically contiguous buildings, the Moslem mosque and the temple of Jagannath at Puri.

—— Edward Thomson: *Rabindranath Tagore: Poet and Dramatist*, Radhi-India Edition, Calcutta, 1979, p. 281.

cultural activities. In his own words,

> The ultimate aim of pursuit of politics is only to unite the heart of the country. But to consider multifarious arrangements for attracting only the foreign hearts by leaving the language and custom of the country to be the highly beneficial political education has only been introduced in a hapless country of ours.
>
> If we admit to win the heart of the society as the highest attainment, then the activities to which we have already been accustomed in ordinary mode of living should be kept apart and the avenues that are eternally open for approaching the country in reality should be brought to light before us. Suppose, if we would appoint our provincial conference to the indigenous strategies in reality, then what would we do? Then, instead of arranging a meeting in the foreign pattern, we would have arranged a meeting of the indigenous one. There the people of the country would congregate from distant places in *Yatras*, songs, festivals and entertainment. An exhibition of indigenous commodities and agricultural products would take place there. Good performers of *kathak*, *kirtan* singers and teams of *Yatra* performers would be rewarded there. The masses would be advised on theories of health and hygiene through magic lanterns etc. there and whatever we would like to say, whatever we would like to advise on weal and woe would have been discussed togther irrespective of persons gentle or not, in simple Bengali language.

—— Rabindranath Tagore: "*Swadeshi Samaj*" ("The Indigenous Society"), *Rabindra-Rachanavali*, Government of West Bengal, Calcutta. Tagore Birth Centenary Edition. 1961 Vol. XII. pp. 687-688.

[Translated by me.

Moreover, as Rabindranath wants to disseminate education among all sections of people in the society, he approaches the most psychological avenue in order to arrive at the desirable point of success in social development and social consciousness. It is to make education simple, cheap and easily available to one and all. This is one of the fundamental reasons why he emphasizes a great deal on revival of ancient Indian and indigenous system of education that incorporates *yatra, kathakata, kirtan* etc. that have immense impression upon the social and cultural life of the masses. The recitals from the *Ramayana* and the *Mahabharata* made in conformity with the spread of mass education in social congregations in the past in our country had definitely moulded the emotional, intell ectual and social minds of the masses and these have their roles even now to bring about desirable social development. That is why Tagore makes an earnest appeal to understand and appreciate the inner values of introducing the indigenous system of mass education by means of awakening social consciousness in the indirect pattern of dissemination of education of ancient times.*

* Dr. H.B. Mukherjee makes a characteristic analysis of mass education for social awareness as envisaged by *Rabindranath Tagore*

> Tagore also stressed the need of encouraging and reviving the various indigenous forms of mass-education as the means to disseminate the desirable kind of education among the people. He earnestly pleaded for reviving and expanding the network of village *pathsalas* of the traditional type as the starting point for the purpose. He also pointed out the great educative value of the recitation on a mass scale of the epics and the *Ramayana* and the *Mahabharata* and of the *Kirtan* type of music recitals, which had not only provided aesthetic enjoyment through their literary and musical elements but had held aloft before the common

> people the cherished ideals and traditions of the land, that had served to elevate their character and bring strength and solace to their mind in the sorrows and struggles of their day-to-day life. Similarly, he pointed out the great importance that the *mela* type of fairs once used to have in the life of our villagers, because of their numerous interesting exhibits, because of the opportunity for contact with the people of other localities and regions that they used to provide, and because of the occasion that they used to create for lectures and tasks given by noted personalities for the enlightenment and edification of the masses. Tagore contends that these were the more natural and familiar, and hence effective, forms of mass gathering in our country than the new-fangled modes of meetings and conferences which, taken in all, had an exotic air about them and were likely to prove unattractive to the common people.

H.B. Mukherjee: *Education For Fulness*, Asia Publishing House, Bombay. 1962. Ch. XVI. P. 307.

This serves the two-fold purpose of education through indigenous strategies and negotiating proper socialization of every member of the society in a sure and sound manner. This also ensures education for effective social integration. This is not accidental but natural, for education in all civilized countries is a whole-hearted all-embracing affair, where side by side with formal education, the process of education in the informal manner of mass education goes on in spontaneity.

Taking all the above views into serious consideration, Tagore staunchly attacks stereotyped, mechanical, imitative, life-less patterns of education alien from living contacts with the masses and the society. That education is never limited to a few specialized enclosures in the names of schools, colleges, universities and other institutes of learning but is well spread out in the wider circumference of the society where every act of mutual understanding and appreciation, functions and festivals, entertainments and performing arts abundantly contributes to a healthy growth of mind and outlook, is undoubtedly a newer approach to the dissemination of education for mass consciousness towards which Rabindranath aims at the principles and strategies of education in our country as well. His own elucidation on this point deserves mention:

> The word 'education' with which we are satisfied introspectively by reciting it has its appearance of the store-house, but looking outside we encounter the sea of emptiness all around. The lofty lantern has been hung for the light of education in schools and colleges, but if that is a captured light in the closed walls, then we would say that we are unfortunate. A picture manifests throughout the canvas. Likewise, in order to have explicity, education awaits countrywide involvement. That education bereft of its extensive role is so vague and incomplete, its pains of poverty have died down in our mind due to our habits alone. When we compare our country with the other one on education, we only observe the visible part and never make an account of the invisible one. With resemblence, we see there are also universities there; and their replicas in the forms of one or two are also being seen in our country. We forget that there is not a single fortunate country where beyond the stipulated educational institutions there is not a wider circumference well spread throughout the horizon of nonstipulated education embracing the whole society.

—— Rabindranath Tagore : " *Sikshar Vikiran*" (" Dissemination of Education "), *Siksha,* Viśva-Bharati. 1973. p. 214.

[Translated by me.

Rabindranath emphasizes on mass education pri -

marily because formal education attained through schools, colleges and universities fail to reach the masses in the society. What is more aweful is that this visible part of education serves as a constraint to the invisible part which is the feeder of the masses in the society. Therefore, the light of education never reaches down to the masses who remain ignored and rather ostracised in the name of education. The roles of the *pathsalas* and the *toles,* the *chatuspathis* and the diverse entertainment media such as *yatras, kathakatas, kirtans* etc. have all along been stimulating to furtherance of mass education in the society. And, as soon as the country is agog with neo-educational experimentations to boost so called modernity, the healthy atmosphere of dissemination of mass education for social awakening has been severely affected and jeopardised.

When Rabindranath upholds indigenous education by means of spelling out the essential aims and objectives of mass education for social consciousness, he makes an introspective analysis of education in relation to age-old social culture and tradition. The purpose is mainly to signify the role of education among all the people of the society in a natural and spontaneous manner. His own introspective analysis in this context is even now relevant:

> Like the mediaeval era of Europe education, through *sastras* alone was fundamental. The special pursuit of this education was made in *toles* and *chatuspathis* but the role of learning was extended throughout the country. There was a continual exchange between specialized knowledge and general knowledge. There was not that antagonistic relationship between the assembly of scholars and unscholarly locality as between an oasis and a desert. There was no part in the country that did not endear the *Ramayana,* the *Mahabharata,* the religious discourses that would regularly spread through

divese channels. Even those theoretical knowledge that are discussed under strenuous perseverance in philosophy were also irrigated in the soil of the minds of the masses all the time. The food for the tree needs to be made liquid so that the tree might take it in all its branches and twigs. In the same way, serious learning in those days has been simplified and disseminated among the minds of the masses. When public work was a part of religion in our country, the arrangements for reservoirs of water at every village were extensive by nature. To quench thirst arrangements for water were spontaneously made by all together. There was no need for appealing to the spend-thrift personnels of the royal court for water. In the same way, society has disseminated indigenous learning in spontaneity. Otherwise the whole country would turn into cruelly black barbarities. Learning then was not a property of the learned, that was a property of the whole society.

— *Ibid.* pp. 214-215

[Translated by me.

To make education universal and all pervasive in the society, what Tagore wants to revitalize is the spirit of mutual understanding between the learned and the ignorant, the enlightened and the non-enlightened masses in the society. The vastness of the society as well as the country from a broader perspective of vision necessitates vastness of approach to education, and this is what Rabindranath emphasizes in course of his own strategies for mass education. This type of education which in course of time has been lightly termed as popular education is never an alienated, sugarcoated, patchwork type of education nor is it education of the inferior type. He always denounces class-oriented, segregated, sub standard type of education in the name of mass education which has with the advent of westernized education, been suffering from the standpoint of quality. Perhaps Rabindranath for the first time does not allow any difference between mass education or for that end in view popular education and higher learning from the qualitative point of view. The difference, according to him, lies only in degree. Hence, higher learning for the masses in the society for awakening of all embracing social consciousness. Education in the real sense of the term must be education for all and must not be limited to the learned few of the society. And true education has its deep rooted effects upon all stratas of the society that in communion rebuilds and reinforces the country. Tagore further accentuates mass education and hightens it from the standpoint of creativity and aesthetic consciousness which amply contribute to education for social emancipation. In fact, in case of advancement of education and for advancement of humanism as well, he has strong objection to the concept of 'common people' which allows to thrive the sense of social disintegration and disunity. Thus he brings forth a new role of popular education as an aid to dissemination of mass education enriched qualitatively and at the same time introduces a newer avenue of mass education by means of encouraging creative and aesthetic education which is even now being dwarfed and overshadowed by materialistic, utiltarian, computerized education. Moreover, the so-called common people greatly contribute to the advancement of the society like the so-called people of the elite classes --an experience that Tagore thankfully encounters while he makes a tour to Russia and thereafter puts it in practice in his own educational experimentations at Santiniketan and Sriniketan:

> Meagre and partial education he regarded as no education at all. Whether it was meant for the rural or the urban population,for the poor or the rich. Education, for whomsoever it is meant, must, therefore, be education in the real sense, as he conceived of it. Popular

education, Tagore insisted, should differ from the higher learning in a country in degree only, but not in quality; what knowledge is gathered at the higher levels from various sources should water down to the lower levels all over that land. That is why, he considered it essential that the core of the new learning acquired from the West at the universities should disseminate among the masses in forms intelligible and interesting to them, and the benefit of the western sciences and technology should be made available to all and sundry, so that the country as a whole might march with the times and reap the fruits of advancement of knowledge in the cultural as well as the material sphere. He was equally insistent that the aesthetic side of the life of the villagers and the common people should be fully attended to by giving them regular training in the fine arts and crafts as well as in art-appreciation, and by encouraging their creative activities in the different forms of art, music and dancing in the old and the new traditions, so that their life might partake of the joy and beauty which had hitherto been open only to a fortunate few. This was another thing that had profoundly impressed the poet in course of his Russian tour. The Russians provided education for the entire populace on a full scale; there was no reservation whatsoever for any class in this matter. The curriculum and activities in the People's Schools and the Pioneers' Communes had been most generously conceived, and as such stress laid on training in the finer arts and aesthetic appreciation as on scientific and technological education. "What is noteworthy", Tagore wrote,, " is that they do not want to bring up the common people on the refuse of the higher classes. They have hundred

> per cent facilities in respect of education, comfort, and the amenities of life. It is so mainly because there are no people here except the common people. In the book of life they do not form mere appendices; they constitute all its chapter"
>
> *(Russia-r chithi. p. 94)*

—— H.B. Mukherjee: *Education For Fulness,* Asia Publishing House, Bombay. 1962. Chapter 16. p. 305.

To bridge the appalling gap between education of the higher classes and that of the common people in our society in order to make a real platform of education for all and sundry in the most effective manner, Tagore specially insists on doing away with the differentiating patterns of education even now nurtured more or less in our country. This is significantly evident in the patterns of education provided for the rural and the urban people in our country. From a casual study of educational opportunities in the society it is undeniable that education has been concerned and geared to the affluent -- a 'buying' commodity as the report of the Kothari Commission of India (1964-66) sadly admits -- and hardly to the common man. The light of education, therefore, fails to reach every nook and corner of the society. It has also failed to enkindle the social consciousness of all and sundry. A certain sense of social passivity has gravely engulfed the arena of education which has turned out to become something else than education or, better to term it, miseducation. As a psycho-social observer *par excellence,* Rabindranath exposes this grim picture of society -- shy, common-man-ignoring, utilitarian, affluent-prone system of education in a very characteristic manner:

> The education that we call in this era starts in towns. As corrolaries to it business ana service follow it. This foreign process of education is like the light of a railway compartment.

> The compartment is bright but the vast track along which the train is running is covered in darkness. The carriage of the workshop is alone real and the whole country resonant with the pains of life is as if not real.
>
> Banking upon this opportunity a group of people living in towns is blessed with education, esteem, affluence. They alone became enlightened, enkindled. At the backdrop of that light the rest of the country became submerged in total eclipse. Those who learnt lessons on English by heart, sitting on the school bench, under the educated society as the country due to their blindness consequential to educationally enlightened sight, took the wings for a peacock and ivory for an elephant.

——Rabindranath Tagore: " *Sikshar Vikiran* " (" Dissemination of Education"), *Siksha,* Visva-Bharati. 1973. p. 216.

[Translated by me.

The parochial system of education depriving the vast majority of people of access to education pains Tagore so exceedingly that he deplores ivory-aware education *sans* relationship with the whole gamut of the society. Again, the so-called enlightened education that invites complex and denunciation, apathy and deprivation hinders education from being a broadened disseminator of mass awareness to bitter social cohesion. As a matter of fact, this type of education that allows compartmentalism and creates disunity and disintegration is only a patchwork and betrays modernity that ensures dynamism and unity. And so, any type of education that fulfils a parochial aim in view cannot meet the needs of social consciousness--a fact on which Tagore harps to voice his protest against clerk-prone education during the foreign yoke in our country. Side by side with this protest, he also glaringly refers to the deploring condition of primary education in our country, that once significantly contributed to pupils' social awakening, on account of the fact that the greed for westernized education has already overpowered the easily trapped intelligentsia and the inevitable outcome is that the neo-educational approach to education at the early stage is heavily burdened with matters related to foreign culture, foreign society and foreign environmental informatics. The most harmful aspect, above all, is the closure of mass media which were so long nourished by means of arrangements of healthy social entertainments like the *yatras* the *kirtans* and so on. The pulsating spirit of social nearness that provides a sustenance of life socially and culturally was synchornized in the mass education programmes very effectively. Moreover, a healthy growth of the society in such types of social functions and festivals as above assured education for joy and fulness of life. Even administrative machineries of the country often overpowered by alien culture and tradition somehow or other even now await a rethinking on the fact that social development is more important than bare affluence which is continually eating up the vitalities of human efflorescence. What Tagore essentially intends on revitalization of the society through mass education as it was a perenial practice in ancient India is to bring about a sense of awareness to the fact that thereshould be greater affluence of the food for vibrating social life than for the romantic greed for adventurism in utilitarianism.

To avert adventurism and to arouse the inner spirit of consciousness in each individual is, as Rabindranath firmly advocates, the only way of regeneration of society. Education acts as a tool for such social regeneration and the individual cannot but orient himself by means of his own intelligence, his own heartfelt experiences and by his own tastes and temperaments. How to make every individual in the society self-conscious, strong, dynamic? How to boost him to believe that he is not as he is, but he should be as true to his own self as to others? Education must steer him towards that avenue of awareness. And if, on the other hand, education turns out to be a means of bare living alone as mechanical education compels, life is actually lost in nothingness. The social responsibilities cannot be left aside, for a society with so-called educated persons living on drabness and abstraction becomes a number or a tool bereft of the real joy of conjoint, communicated, thriving social life.

When Tagore speaks of indigenous society he badly intends to visualize in reality the spontaneous growth of the society in the education of self-esteem, self-development and self-culture amidst social relationsips in diverse dimensions. Let education be turned into real social involvement in which an individual grows both within and in the midst of others to taste the beyonding of experience and erudition, poignance and devotion. Let every mind be stimulated with knowledge and appreciation, enquiry and askance in every aspect of social development. This will also assure unity of mind which will prize humanity with the essence of creative unity- the most coveted prize that education sincerely awaits and offers. In elucidating social freedom and for that end in view social emancipation, Tagore inspires stimulation of mass education to safeguard mankind against cowardice and parasitic attitude. He characteristically refers to the sense of social responsibility of our countrymen who, in spite of alien administration, shouldered all responsibilities of education, health and hygiene, religion, hospitality and diverse social entertainment programmes. All the activities related to mass education were organized in a very routine-oriented, systematized, disciplined manner; while renovation of ponds and canals were made, health programmes related to educate the masses on mosquitoes, contagious diseases, drinking water, nursing, child care and so on attracted the attention of every person in the society. The current of humanity enriched in the education of social consciousness became all-pervading only because there was an inherent social linkage between man and man, which in the backdrop of the modern relationship between the rural and the urban society necessitates reintroduction in Tagorean social perspectives. To be more explicit, it is better to refer to Rabindranath's view-points on the role of the *melas* or social gatherings that have a great educative value and bears relevance even now:

> Our country is primarily rural oriented. When these villages become enthusiastic now and then to feel in their pulses the blood circulation of the big world outside, then fairs alone are the way out. These fairs beckon the outer world inside. in those festivals, villages become free from all pettiness: this is the fundamental scope for contributing whole-heartedly and for accepting others. As the advent of the rains is to fill in the tanks with the water from the sky, so the appropriate scope for filling in the hearts of the villages is the fair.
>
> This fair is very natural in our country. If you call on the countrymen in connection with a meeting, they will attend fearfully; it will take a long time to open out their minds. But when all congregate together on the occasion of a fair, they easily come with open hearts. And so the real scope to win the mind of the country becomes available. When the villagers have taken leave by discontinuing cultivation, then alone is the time to sit beside them.
>
> There is not a single district in Bengal when in the different period of the year and at different places fairs are not held. First, it is our duty to collect a list and an account of these fairs. Afterwards we should take records to be rightly acquainted with the people of the country in connection with these fairs.
>
> If, in every district, the gentle and edu-

> cated community can awaken their fairs anew and invigorate in new hearts afresh, if the educated persons of the country infuse their hearts into these fairs, if they establish good relationship among the Hindus and the Muslims in these fairs, make consultations for eradicating the lacuna of the district in relation to schools, conveyances, tanks, cultivated lands etc. leaving off all connections with barren politics, then within a very short time, they can really turn out the country to be dynamic.

—— Rabindranath Tagore: "*Swadeshi Samaj*", *Rabindra Rachanavali*, Government of West Bengal, Calcutta, Tagore Birth Centenary Edition, 1911, Vol. XII, p. 688.

[Translated by me.

To revive the rural fairs, as Tagore visualizes, is not only to usher forth a new era of economic and social consciousness but along with this to allow all persons in the society to consolidate the relationship of the heart. Men in the society come closer to each other only when there is mutual understanding and appreciation. As an introspective social thinker, Tagore strongly advocates for revival of the inner current of joy and appreciation in every person living in the society. The dry heart of the country awaits a drenched shower of joy and pleasure, unity and appreciation which would endlessly ignite the social sensibilities that are more or less becoming blunt or utterly undergoing stress and strain as a complex society naturally encounters.

With a view to revitalizing the spirit of social oneness, Rabindranath intends to disseminate the spirit of united endeavour by means of education of self-dependence and sincerity of purpose. He negotiates the charges against rural fairs about its association with pseudo-religious activities and upholds the great educative value derived out of it to make the masses conscious of the significance of humanity. As he explicitly remarks:

> We will have to remember this that the big tanks which provided us with water and health and have not only caused water scarcity by being polluted but are also doling out disease and death. In the same way, the fairs that are in vogue in the name of religion in our country have in most cases not only become unfit for mass education by being gradually polluted today, but have also turned out to be an organ of ill education. In the neglected cornfields crops are not being grown and thorns are growing. Under such circumstances, if we do not revive these fairs as sponsors of ugly entertainments, we would be guilty to our own country and religion.

—— Rabindranath Tagore: "*Swadeshi Samaj*", *Rabindra Rachanavali*, Government of West Bengal, Calcutta, Tagore Birth Centenary Edition, 1961. Vol. XII, p. 689.

[Translated by me.

Toreorient mass education as a great social synchronizer of mankind, is, as Tagore emphasizes, the only way to foster the spirit of unity and joy amidst man. It is also to drive away the evil aspects of the social modes of living and superstition even now looming large in social customs and entertainments. Moreover, with the minium exposure of littleness of mind and outlook, the sufferings of the society are, indeed, legion. These can only be eliminated when each person in the society makes himself responsible for loss of patience and insincerity of purpose. These can only be negotiated when education plays its vital role among the masses in the society to be introspective and honest to contribute to the society as best as possible. Rabindranath, of course, gives primary importance to self-study which would enable everyone in the society to continually and actively maintain a cordial relationship between man and man. This cordiality as he forewarns, should be safeguarded against greed and peevishness of mind. Unless one is strong enough both from moral as well as aesthetic points of view, education in the society hardly serves its purpose successfully, and unless an all-embracing consciousness of humanity pervades in the society whatsoever and howsoever it might be, the society concerned suffers a great deal from the whims and caprices of a few persons with vested interests or from undue 'isms' and -ites' that profusely eat up the life-blood of a society. Education, then, should amass mass force not apparently and quantitatively but introspectively and qualitatively to bring about fruitful social revolution.

Unlike other social thinkers harbouring on affluence and immediate gain of the society by means of affluence and utilitarianism by ignoring exposures of the inner social attributes of mankind, Tagore continually stresses on unity of mankind through inner efflorescence of social consciousness where education plays a very significant role. The lesson of unison of mutual social sensibilities crystallized through education is the only lesson for regeneration of humanism. As a social being, man cannot keep himself apart from innumerable problems, and as problems are there--social, economic or otherwise--he cannot but entrust himself with the arduous duty of evolving newer and worthier avenues of negotiating with them. Rabindranath always makes us aware of the fact that as a social being, every one of us should wholeheartedly endeavour to be united for a strong battle against the diverse ills of the society. For him as for everyone of us, education serves as the lone armour to bring about a radical approach to social unity which strengthens each individual to wage an endless war against all deficiencies and weaknesses in regard to social and global responsibilities. The hunger for truth is, as he says, the greatest social hunger and the masses can be revitalized to alleviate this hunger only when education is given its proper due in the society. The history of man as a social being awaits to be rewritten in its march for victory against all odds and constraints of social development. It is more than apparent independence which Tagore denounces as superficial because it does not essentially help but hinders when the masses, *sans* education, are deprived of the freedom and unity of mind and the heart in the society. In his poignant and invaluable analysis of man and civilization from the socio-humanistic points of view, he refers to the inner social vision of mankind awaiting appropriate awareness to union of mind and outlook:

> Every nation embraces within itself why it stands for and the special problems it confronts. With ceaseless endeavour, it has to fulfil its inner worth. With this endeavour alone, it creates its character and its innovative power is emboldened. Man is to win his humanity at every moment. The history of every nation is the history of its own march for victory. Its health and its wealth lie in eliminating difficult obstacles. For this, it is said: fortune favours the brave. Man has made the inaccessible accessible and unattainable attainable. A particular nation as it is involved in a particular problem by the Almighty, finds its way out in giving true reply to it. Those who have failed to solve are undone. And those who have thought that there is nothing to solve and everything has been solved have alone become distressed. So long as there is life in man there are problems for him. His process of living is to ceaselessly giving answers to problems. All around, there are continual constraints of the non-living. To continually challenge these constraints is to prove that life is. ****** The fundamental principle of the human society is the unity of man. Civilization means practice of mankind to be united.

> Wherever the realization of this theory of unity is weak the country is entangled with that weakness in forms of manifold diseases and is attacked from all around.

——— Rabindranath Tagore:"*Bharatpathik Rammohan Roy*", *Rabindra Rachanavali*, Government of West Bengal, Calcutta, Tagore Birth Centenary Edition, 1961. Vol. XI, p. 384.

[Translated by me.

Keeping in mind the inner social vision of mankind, Rabindranath himself experiments upon disseminating education among the masses by means of highlighting education through the mother tongue. Learning a foreign language and apeing foreign social culture and environment affect a lot in efflorescence of true humanism. Moreover, with the introduction of an alien language the emergence of the elite society becomes inevitable. The birth of neo-intellectuals in our own country by depriving the vast masses who remain poor and illiterate, ignored and unprivilieged points towards the erosion of social awareness that characterizes a humane society. Tagore emphasizes on mass education through the mother tongue not merely to heighten and glorify the prestige of the language concerned but also for invigorating the spirit of freedom of mind and worth of social awareness.

Admittedly, when Tagore reminds us that the mother tongue is like the milk of the mother, he emphasizes on mass education to renew the approach to enkindle social awareness in the light of receiving the new world of knowledge and experience in tune with a fresh approach to society. The indigenous approach to learning has its deep-rooted effects upon the minds of the masses. As a social Psycho-analyst, Rabindranath considers it to be the most important duty of every socio-educational thinker to arouse and educate the mind of every person in the society. How to educate the minds of the masses? The answer, as he is very explicit, is to allow every person in the society to think in terms of a simile. Just as a tree is emancipated from the sapling and the sapling from its seed, so the human society is liberated from the individual and the individual from his womb of thoughts and imaginations absolutely of his very own. Education, and nothing else, serves its best purpose to arouse the intellectual fervour and the innate strength of the mind of an individual. The task of a social educator is, as he strongly suggests, to educate the mind of man as a social being--the social man, so to say--very carefully and cautiously, and this cannot be performed without the help of the mother-tongue. That he discourages introduction of any foreign language for growth of national mind and social outlook is only because even if there might be some sort of advancement of the society be it in the form of mass education non-formally or in that of formal education in schools, colleges etc., whatsoever, it will in the long run prove futile as it would create a totally artificial social atmosphere giving ample berths to segregation, secessionism, class-distinction, apathy and hatred in the society. What Rabindranath considers to be a glaring defect of mass education through the medium of a foreign language is even now ignored: it is that with our endeavour at encouraging education for social emancipation by means of a foreign language there might be a more or less broadening of the mind but then the language of our own that is the mother-tongue with which we should fundamentally be enriched from the psycho-social points of view will be severely affected. This is evident because our medium of thought and expression finds its most favourable atmosphere in the mother-tongue alone and when this is ignored, education in any dimension--particularly mass education--becomes cancerous and parasitic. What is peculiarly seen in the society is a two-fold behavioural approach and pattern of the alien language bred and sustained 'social' man who learns a language in one situation and leaves mother-tongue aside to be alienated from himself as well as from the society. Whither social consciousness?

Education *sans* social consciousness amongst the masses is, as Rabindranath earnestly believes, no education at all. To ostracize society from the so--called educated few is to ostracize humanity, and when education is geared to this end in view, it turns into miseducation inviting incoherence and chaos in the minds of the masses. To eliminate the evils of education as above, Tagore for the first time introduces a new institution for dissemination of mass education for social consciousness in 1936. He christens it as *Loka-Siksha Samsad* (Public Education Society). The purpose of the institution is more clearly analysed in terms of education at home and during leisure hours for anyone anywhere. Low priced books on health, hygiene, science, literature, arithmetic, general knowledge, history, geography, elementary Hindi catering to social needs and temperaments and written in Bengali at different levels bring forth a very worthy divident in mass education. Tagore himself takes a strong initiative to introduce in Bengali different types of text-books under *Loka-Siksha Granthamala* series written by eminent scholars at his personal request to meet the thirst for knowledge of the common people. Moreover, he also acquaints the masses with the vast treasure-world of knowledge and experience of the western thinkers through well-translated versions in Bengali in the *Visva -- Vidya Samgraha* series which are in conformity with books of the Home University Library series.

A great disseminator of popular science among the masses, Tagore inspires education in science for highlighting a scientific approach to social awareness. The books patronized by him for this end in view are all included in the *Visva-Parichay* series and they cover a wide arena of science education in simple, easy to understand Bengali language. His own *Visva-Parichay,* a book on science written just four years before his death, shows how he is greatly interested in bringing about social consciousness in the most appropriate scientific perspectives. The genesis of the Open University system in our country owes a lot to his innovative approaches to agriculture, science and technology, which, as a consequence, have moulded the minds of the masses towards better and worthier socialization. His own experiments in connection with practical and physical education at *Siksha-Satra* (The poet's School),*Siksha Charcha, Palli-Samgathan Vibhaga* (Department of Rural Reconstruction) aptly speak of his unfailing endeavour at regenerating new dimensions of social consciousness among the masses. The introduction of rural games and sports through *Brati Balak* organisation which are of the types of Boys' Scouts and Girls' Guides and revival of oriental classical approaches to physical education for social discipline and social security like the Japanese Judo, Karate, Kong-fu etc. by inviting experts show how keen he is in updating the education of the masses for social excellence.

From a study of Tagore as an emancipator of mass education for social consciousness it might seem to us that he has been greatly influenced by western thinkers. Be that as it may, but, above all, it is undeniable that as a creative social thinker who considers the soul-force as the most dynamic strategy of bringing about social regeneration, he always remains as an unparalleled and distinctive visionary. When today's education particularly at the school level frantically seeks the most effective and ideal avenue of dissemination of social awareness, let us ponder over it in the light of the true social perspective of Rabindranath right now or never:

> What should be the role of the school in relation to social progress, it is asked; whether the school should play, as the essentialists maintain, a conservative role and foster the cherished ideals and traditions of the community; or whether it should perform, as the pragmatists advocate, only a critical role, criticizing the current trends in the society as well as the plans for social reconstruction put forward by the state, while refraining from presenting any concrete plan of its own, or whether it should

play, as the Progressives desire, a creative role, not merely criticizing in a negative way,but producing dynamic creative forces in the society with concrete plans of its own for social progress, or whether it should go still further and play, as the Marxists would have it, a positively revolutionary role, fomenting the destructive revolutionary forces in the society in order to construct a new social order in place of the old; or whether it should remain completely neutral, avoiding all controversies and concentrating only on the pursuit of knowledge? It is difficult to place Tagore entirely in anyone of the above categories. His position, as in most cases, is a synthesis of all these approaches. Like the conservatives, he desired that educational institution should not be uprooted from their precious past heritage but should reflect the cherished ideals of the community. Like the pragmatists,he desired that the schools should encourage independent rational thinking. He had even advocated the revolutionary role once during the Swadeshi Movement of 1905, when he had exhorted the students to give up their studies at a time of national crisis and join the forces of liberation. But later on, he changed his position, and somewhat on the lines of the Neutralists, strongly warned that Santiniketan should be completely aloof from all political turmoil and concentrate on the dispassionate pursuit of knowledge and truth. But his general position appears to have been more in sympathy with the creative role than with the rest. He did not go to the extent of advocating outright indoctrination, but certainly desired that the schools should adopt a dynamic creative role in building a new and better social order.

------ H. B. Mukerjee : *Education for Fulness,* Asia Publishing House, Bombay 1962. Chapter 16 pp. 309-310.

Do we ever encounter more creative and dynamic social thinker of mass education than Rabindranath?

3

EDUCATION FOR SOCIO AESTHETIC EXCELLENCE

TAGOREAN GUIDELINES

Education comprises the individual as well as the society. For education in the real sense of the term it necessitates something more. It is to seek excellence both within an individual and in the society. What kind of excellence should education seek? Should it revive the essence of age-old indigenous values and culture, tradition and heritage, a sense of individual or social patterns of life, ideas and ideals or should it bring about a radical approach to society and man as a newer pathfinder of individual and social efflorescence? Should it arouse a far more modern approach to individual and social concepts of the inner development of the society and its clienteles modern in the sense that it brushes aside all the apparently abstract nuances and finer sensibilities which are undesirably very essential to the growth and development of the inner man to be a worthy contributor to the growth and development of the society as well and pays more attention to so-called practicalities and modernities that mesmerize humanity to forge ahead with the romantic vision of individual and social transformation either in abstractions of utiliterianism or in utter vainglories of super-science and mega-automations? Should it enlighten man and society to see steadily and see within the serene images of man and society in absolute perfection and poignance as the true spiritual thinker of the world always strives for or should it march for an individual and social millennia surging ahead with a yet-too-vague and ticklish sentimental delirium of socio-aesthetics that would fulfil the vision of a classless society as the marxists boldly dig out as the outcome of human intelligentsia? Should it endeavour at allowing man and the society to share together the ethical and the moral values derived out of the rich and varied experiences of Nature, the greatest teacher of socio-aesthetics or should it allow man and the society to encage all naturalists in the whirlpool of scientific and technological marvels and fillip the crazy atmosphere of man and society to enjoy the death-dance by becoming victims to schizophrenic mechanomania?

'On the threshold of a new era of the socio-aesthetic transformation and changes in human behavioural designs, Rabindranath upholds the classical view of socio-aesthetics and endears education as the most significant and vital force to bring about lasting changes in men and society. With vast experience of men from all walks of life as a penetrative socio-aesthetic thinker and visualizer while he was engaged in contact with the masses at Shilaidah and Patisar in undivided Bengal (now in Bangladesh), he enriched himself with manifold experiences of man and society in relation to aesthetic development. This undoubtedly ensured him to renew his vision of the social man who might educate himself with all the essential aesthetic sensibilities as revealed in deverse interactions in the society. Already, with colonial education dwarfing the inner aesthetic visions of man and the society, he himself was painfully aware; but the social constraints did not allow him to translate his own socio-aesthetic viewpoints in reality. As a practical socio-aesthetic thinker, Tagore harmonizes education to Nature as well as to life. This has added a new dimension to education as a living force for man's development of socio-aesthetic sensibilities. In his treatise on the dubious role of education in our country, entitled "The Vicissitudes of Education" ----*Sikshar Herpher* --- his first essay on the problem of education, presented exactly a century ago at a public meeting in Rajshahi (Now in Bangladesh) and published in the Visva-Bharati Quarterly (November-January, 1947) under the title "Topsy-turvy Education", he strongly advocates for feeling the socio-aesthetic pulse of the country through education and this, he suggests as a very practical thinker, can be most successfully felt only when education is imparted through the mother-tongue. For emancipation of the man sophisticated in social as well as aesthetic sensibilities, he urges on allowance of the breadth of vision in education instead of being crippled in alien language, mechanical learning, bare passing in a few so-called examinations and exercise of foreign culture and tradition. His own exposition is a telling one:

> Human beings cannot be content with the bare necessaries of life, and they are in fact partly chained to their needs and partly free. The average man is three and a half cubits tall, but he lives in a house that is much taller, and has plenty of room for the freedom of movement so essential for health and comfort. This applies equally to education. A boy should be allowed to read books of his own choice: in addition to the prescribed text-books he must read for his school-work. His mental development is likely to be arrested if he is not allowed to do this, and he may grow into a man with the mind of a boy.

> Unfortunately, a boy in this country has very little time at his disposal. He must learn a foreign language, pass several examinations, and qualify himself for a job, in the shortest possible time. So, what can he do but cram up a few text-books with breathless speed? His parents and his teachers do not let him waste precious time by reading a book at entertainment, and they snatch it away from him the moment they see him with one.

——Rabindranath Tagore: "The Vicissitudes of Education", *Towards Universal Man,* Asia Publishing House,1961. p.1.

For a society truly elevated to aesthetic excellence, education indeed plays a very significant role. Unlike other social thinkers, Tagore makes an inroad adventure to bring about a radical change of socialism by allowing aesthetics to have its proper place in the society. The cultivation of the mother-tongue towards that direction is aimed at emancipation of socio-aesthetic sensibilities towards desirable and worthwhile perfection. Let the functions and the festivals of the society going on from time immemorial be revived and oriented with a little touch of aesthetic excellence. Let the sense of serenity and poignance be allowed to adorn all social reactions, habits, customs and tradition. Let the cultural components of the society be honoured and practised with all dignity and sophistication. Let every act of morality and values be crystallized with aesthetic patterns of human endeavour. Tagore's own process of teaching children to be equipped with a conscious mind instead of taxing them with dry matters for so-called advancement of knowledge, and allowing children to be in close contact with the beauty and mystery of nature in order to develop their unparalleled sense of aesthetics and appreciation, values and sociabilities is very significant as it is born in the womb of his own experiences as a school boy, and later on as a teacher:

I had at least acquired a negative experience in the course of my own school days. I had learnt how not to treat children. What I had particularly suffered in my childhood was to feel that the education that I had received was separated from life. I admit I had a certain special sensibility which others did not share with me in the same degree, otherwise I would undoubtedly have more easily resigned myself to my suffering, and would, in the course of those days at school, have succeeded like the others in stifling in me that passionate zest for life, for nature, from which everyday I had to be dragged away as from a mother in order to enter the classroom.

I recall it, the door of the classroom, gaping each morning like a big mouth, its bare walls, its wooden benches, its wooden desk at which the teacher stood giving his lesson like a living phonograph. I still know it by heart, and I can hear it, the repetition of the same, which had neither the beauty of melody nor rhythm, which every morning we chanted in chorus on the wooden verandah of the school before entering the class. It spoke of many good things no doubt; that it was necessary to be wise, not to steal, nor borrow. But it was, nevertheless, a bad beginning for the day.

* * * * * *

It was not, however, that I believed that I had any special gift for teaching, but it seemed to me that I had the secret of making them (children) happy.

To tell you the truth, nobody had any faith in me. I had neither a university degree, nor distinction of any kind. I passed for an extremely unpractical hand, who knew nothing except writing verse. It was now a matter of finding blankets and sheets and of procuring food and lodging for the five boys who had been entrusted to my care.

I tried to live their daily life. Education, properly speaking, was a secondary matter-what was of the first importance was that our life was lived in common--our comradeship.

For me, indeed, a child up to his twelfth year lives much more in the sub-conscious than in clear consciousness and what is important during these first years is not to burden his memory with knowledge which taxes his mind, but to see that his subconscious is saturated with beauty through the contact of living nature.

——— Rabindranath Tagore: 'A poet's school', *March of India*, March-April 1951 (Delhi), Translated by Sasadhar Sinha from "L, Educateur" No. 12, June 11, 1921, Quoted from *Social Thinking of Rabindranath Tagore*, Asia Publishing House, Bombay 1962. pp. 149-150.

What is the strategy of Tagore's teaching which might direct us to be socio-aesthetic in our approach to education? What are his significant points of departure from others? An iconoclast in the arena of education, he strongly protests against burdening children with a curriculum that eats up the living visions of unfolding themselves both socially as well as aesthetically to be buoyant with the spirit of freedom and love amidst nature. As he categorically observes:

When I teach anything, I always do it

with love. I put myself heart and soul into it. And my friends tell me: "you could have obtained the same result with less effort; children must be given nourishment in rationed portions such as canned food". I know it well. But that is to kill the mind. We have had to do it in our own school also. But I know that I am guilty of a crime. I hope that I shall be forgiven this in the other world, because truly I am not responsible for it alone. I have committed the crime in spite of myself.

* * * * * *

Thus one leading principle, and one only, emanates from my ideas: Go to meet life where it is supreme. Come out of the school room. Take the classes out under the trees. Undoubtedly, it is easy to have a tree trunk in the school room, it can be cut up into planks; but these planks are dead, it is not in classroom that the tree will bear flowers and fruits.

Do not be pre-occupied with method. Leave your instincts to guide you to life. Children differ from one another. One must learn to know them, to know them to navigate among them as one navigates among reefs. To explore the geography of their minds, a mysterious instinct, sympathetic to life, is the best of all guides.

– Ibid. pp. 152-153.

To allow pupils to study by themselves their minds which as Tagore describes as 'a mysterious instinct' is yet a far cry in our educational plans and programmes and, as such, the wails of the socio-aesthetic minds of the pupils remain unattended and uncared for even now with object passivity and disinterestedness. Obviously, when it is said that education fails to contribute abundantly to the aesthetic development of the society where 'I' is a lonely and hopeless 'I' and each 'We' is a combination of haphazard and furstrated 'I'-s, the inherent truth is that there is neither any organised and truly educated society nor is there any cultivation or nurturing of aesthetic sensibilities among the people in the society. But this is diametrically opposite to the age-old Indian custom and tradition running in the conjoint communicated and aesthetically enriched society, and when Tagore wants to revive the spirit of the *tapovana* he wants to revive the spirit of simplicity and earnestness, austerity and serenity, modesty and magnanimity. The poem that he wants to write by means of introducing the ancient ashramic atmosphere of *tapovana* 'a fantastic anachronism' as, indeed, it appears today, is a poem in the tangible language of socio-aesthetic excellence in education. True to his own unique way of appreciation, he makes a historical outline for advocating such a serene system in his own school at Santiniketan as follows:

> Civilised man has come far away from the orbit of his normal life. He has gradually formed and intensified some habits, that are likely those of the bees, for adapting himself to his live-world. We so often set modern man suffering from *ennui*, from world-weariness, from a spirit of rebellion against their environment for no reasonable cause whatever. Social revolutions are constantly ushered in with a suicidal violence that has its origin in our dissatisfaction with our hive-wall arrangement--the too exclusive enclosure that deprives us of the perspective, which is so much needed to give us the proper proportion in our art of living. All this is an indication that man has not really been moulded in the model of the bee, and therefore he becomes racklessly anti-social when his freedom to be more than social is

ignored.

> Under our highly complex modern condition, mechanical forces are organised with such efficiency that the materials grow far in advance of man's selective and assimilative capacity to simplify them into harmony with his nature and needs. Such an intemperate overgrowth of things, like the rank vegetation of the tropics, creates confinement for man. The nest is simple, it has an easy relationship with the sky; the cage is complex and costly, it is too much itself, excommunicating whatever lies outside. And modern man is busy building his cage, fast developing his parasitism on the monster, *thing*, which he allows to envelop him on all sides. He is always occupied in adapting himself to its dead angularities, limits himself to its limitations, and merely becomes a part of it.

—— Rabindranath Tagore: "A Poet's School", *Visva-Bharati Quarterly*, Shantiniketan, October 1926. p.200.

To emancipate the self from the clutches of the *thing* and to be in tune with the ideal atmosphere of aesthetic poignance where the learner becomes a partner to sociable trails of behavioural designs as modelled in the *tapovana* Tagore makes an indepth analysis of humane sensibilities contributing abundantly to social excellence. To be 'natural with nature and human with human society', he, therefore, wants to revive 'the missing paradise' in his own school where children might have exercised their creative and aesthetic sensibilities apart from 'any orthodox material, prescribed measure, or standard value'. How is it that in a busy, hurry, crazy, commercial and computerized society the ideal of the *tapovana* system of education catering to pupils' socio-aesthetic and creative development would successfully work?

Even Tagore has the apprehension that the concept of *tapovana* in the context of the present age with all its bizarre conditions of life would pose as 'a fantastic anachronism', but, then, the poem for pupils' socio-aesthetic and all round creative and critical development necessitates writing in a plausible language". That is why he strongly urges for inculcating the spirit of *tapovana* which would bring forth a serene and sombre atmosphere for socio-aesthetic excellence. As he suggest in course of his critical appreciation to *Meghaduta* by Kalidas, a poet suffering from 'the nostalgia' of the soul .

> The poet in the royal courtlived in exile, as it were. It was, he knew, not merely his own exile but that of the whole age to which he was born, the age that had amassed wealth and well-being, and lost its background of the great universe. What was the image in which his desire of perfection persistently appeared in his poems and dramas? It was *tapovana*, the forest resort of the patriarchal community of ancient India. Those who are familiar with Sanskrit literature know that this was not a colony of people with a primitive culture. They were seekers of truth, for the sake of which they lived in purity but not puritanism; they led a simple life, but not one of self-mortification. They did not advocate celibacy and were in close touch with people who pursued worldly interests. Their aim was briefly suggested in the Upanishad in these lines:
>
> *Te sarvagam sarvatah prapya dhira*
> *yuktat manah sarvamevavisanati.*
>
> Those men of serene mind enter into the All, having realized and being everywhere in union with the omnipresent Spirit.
>
> — *Ibid* . pp. 199-200 .

Paying sincere respect to the rich Indian heritage of socio-aesthetic development, Tagore also ardently believes in the philosophy of fulfilment through harmony with nature' that nourishes freedom and individuality. To give a fitting reply to the doled out brick-and-mortar oriented life and to allow children to nurture freshness of senses for easy and natural communication with others in the society, he promotes education of harmony with the whole universe. Here is a poignant description of his own school that would cultivate, with a backdrop of his own reminiscence, the 'power of quick communication':

> Looking back upon those moments of my boyhood when all my mind seemed to float poised upon a large feeling of the sky, of the light, I cannot help believing that my Indian ancestry has left deep in my being the legacy of its philosophy, the philosophy which speaks of fulfilment through harmony with nature. It arouses in us a great desire to seek our freedom, not in the man-made world but in the depth of the universe; and it makes us offer our reverence to the divinity inherent in fire, water and trees, in everything moving and growing. The founding of my school had its origin in the memory of that longing for freedom, the memory which seems to go back beyond the sky-line of my birth.
>
> Freedom in the mere sense of independence is meaningless. Perfect freedom lies in the harmony of relationship which we realised not through *knowing*, but in *being*. Objects of knowledge maintain an infinite distance from us who are the knowers. For knowledge is not union. We attain the world of freedom only through perfect sympathy.

> Children with the freshness of their senses come directly to the intimacy of this world. This is the first great gift they have. They must accept it naked and simple and never lose their power of quick communication. For our perfection we have to be at once savage and civilized; we must be natural with nature and human with human society.
>
> — *Ibid* . pp. 203-204.

To be 'natural with nature and human with human society' as Tagore advocates for an ideal socio-aesthetic development, necessitates a radical approach to education that must challenge stupid bigotry and moral cowardliness. Stereotyped education mutilating social and aesthetic sensibilities is no education, for it aims at artificialities and crudities of life. Being disgusted with the city bred education which has engulfed all finer visions of pupils' aesthetic and social thoughts, he creates Sikaha-Satra, " A Poet's School" as he christens it, where a band of spirited tender boys of the adjacent rural areas come to be educated with socio-aesthetic enrichment. Let the rural society and the rural environment be given a new lease of life freed from all shackles of materialism and utilitarianism. Let them be made socially and aesthetically aware of the pollution in education due to undesirable encroachment of dirty politics which are even now eating up the vigor and vitalities of our rural people. Being distressed at the appalling absence of qualitative education that enriches social consciousness and aesthetic sensibilities, Tagore makes a new experiment on education at Siksha-Satra. In a letter to Leonard Knight Elmhirst on December 19, 1937, he writes:

> You know how for a long time I have been cherishing my hope of establishing an ideal centre of education of Sriniketan--an ideal which is not curtailed to the strictest measure of a narrow village environment, which is now

specially set apart to be doled out as famine ration carefully calculated to be just good enough for an emanciated life and dwarfed mentality. It is well-known that the education, which is prevalent in our country is extremely meagre in the spread of its area and barren in its quality. Unfortunately this is all that is available for us, and the artificial standard set up is proudly considered as respectable. Outside the bhadralogue class, pathetic in their struggle for fixing a university label on their names, there is a vast, obscure multitude who cannot even dream of such a costly ambition. With them we have our best opportunity if we know how to use it. There, and there only, can we be free to offer to our country the best kind of all-round culture not mutilated by official dictators. I have generally noticed that when the charitably-minded, city-bred politicians talk of education for the village folk, they mean a little left-over in the bottom of their cup, after diluting it copiously. They are callously unmindful of the fact that the kind and the amount of the food that is needed for mental nourishment must not be apportioned differently according to the social status of those that receive it.

I am therefore all the more keen that Siksha-Satra should justify the ideal I have entrusted to it, and should represent the most important function of Sriniketan in helping students to the attainment of manhood complete in all its various aspects. Our people need more than anything else a real scientific training that can inspire in them the courage of experiment and the initiative of mind which we lack as a nation. Sriniketan should be able to provide for its pupils an atmosphere of rational thinking

> and behaviour, which alone can save them from stupid bigotry and moral cowardliness. I myself attach much more significance to the educational possibilities of Siksha-Satra than to the school and college at Santiniketan, which are everyday becoming more and more like so many schools and colleges elsewhere in this country, borrowed cages that treat the students' minds as captive birds, whose sole human value is judged according to the mechanical repetition of lessons prescribed by an educational dispensation foreign to the soil.

—— Rabindranath Tagore: "Letter to L.K. Elmhirst" Quoted in *Rabindranather Chintajagat :Siksha Chinta.* Ed. by Satyendranath Roy, Granthalay Private Limited, Calcutta. 1982 pp. 324-325.

How does Rabindranath visualize the role of the villages in fostering the spirit of socialism and aesthetics? How do they teach us the great lesson of humanism? How has a diluted westerinized democracy eaten up, like a demon, all the essence of humane sensibilities and has affected the simple and modest life of the villages? Significantly, Tagore for the first time raises his protest against the rampant "robbery of the soul". He, for the first time, pinpoints how bruised civilization is maimed in fastidious fashion presenting us with an "endless train of respectable rubbish". He also upholds, on the other hand, the healing power of the villages that serve as fountains to the thirsty souls of the modern humanity. As he significantly observes.:

> Civilization has turned into a vast catering establishment. It maintains constant feasts for a whole population of gluttons. The intemperance which could have been tolerated in a few has spread to the multitude. The resulting universal greed is the cause of the meanness,

cruelty and lies in politics and commerce that vitiate the whole human atmosphere. A civilization with an unnatural appetite must feed on numberless victims, and these are being sought in the parts of the world where human flesh is cheap. The happiness of entire peoples in Asia and Africa is being sacrificed to provide fastidious fashion with an endless train of respectable rubbish.

What in the west is called democracy can never be true in a society where greed grows uncontrolled and is encouraged, even admired, by the people. In such an atmosphere a constant struggle goes on among individuals to capture public organizations for their personal ends. Democracy is then like an elephant whose one purpose in life is to give joyrides to the clever and the rich.

Under such conditions the organs through which public opinion is formed together with the machinery of administration are all openly or secretly manipulated by the prosperous few. They have been compared of old to the camel, which can never pass through a needle's eye-the gate that leads to the kingdom of ideals. Such a society is callous and cruel to those who preach their faith in spiritual freedom. In such a society people are intoxicated by the constant stimulation of what they call progress, a progress which they are willing to buy at the cost of civilization itself, like the man for whom wine is more attractive than food.

Villagers are like women. In their keeping is the cradle of the race. They are nearer to

> nature than towns, and in closer touch with the fountain of life. They possess a natural power of healing. It is the function of the village, like that of women, to provide people with this elemental needs, with food and joy, with the simple poetry of life and with those ceremonies of beauty which the village spontaneously produces and in which she finds delight. But when constant strain is upon her, when her resources are excessively exploited, she becomes dull and uncreative. From her time-honoured position of the wedded life, she descends to that of a maid-servent. The city in its intense egotism and pride, remains unconscious of the hurt it inflicts on the very source of its life, health and joy.

—— Rabindranath Tagore: "City and Village", *Towards Universal Man*. Asia Publishing House, Bombay 1961.pp.310-312.

Bearing in mind the appalling sense of apathy and ignorance about the rural people and the rural society where the pulsating sense of beauty and joy reverberates all the time, Tagore goes deep into the inner sense of vision of mankind to revive the old socio-aesthetic norms and values of our country. Consequently, he steers his direction towards a newer discovery of the sub-conscious state of mind of young learners in his own experimental school where the atmosphere is given greater importance than mere rules and methods of instruction. Let the spirit of aesthetics and creativity usher forth in the minds of all learners the endless fountain of beauty and joy in the atmosphere. Let freedom enjoyed by these learners open out newer avenues of social and aesthetic excellence at the same time side by side with economic stability and national prosperity. Let the imagination of the learners be nourished with the "spirit of human relationships" which is more than mere theoretical knowledge of geography. Let there be an open and free cultivation of erudition and understanding of the human minds in close association with diverse avenues of appreciation which would foster sociability and sympathy among children. As Tagore poignantly submits:

> Children have their active sub-conscious mind which, like the tree, has the power to draw food from the surrounding atmosphere. For them the atmosphere is a great deal more important than rules and methods, equipment, text-books and lessons. The earth has her mass of substance in her land and water but, if I may use a figurative language, she finds her stimulus in her atmosphere. It evokes from her responses in colour and perfume, music and movement. In his society man has about himself a diffuse atmosphere of culture. It keeps his mind sensitive to his racial inheritance, to the current of influences that come from tradition; it enables him to imbibe unconsciously the concentrated wisdom of ages. But in our educational organizations we behave like miners, digging only for things and not like the tillers of the earth whose work is a perfect collaboration with nature.
>
> I tried to create an atmosphere in my school--this was the main task. In educational institutions our faculties have to be nourished in order to give our mind its freedom, to make our imagination fit for the world which belongs to art, and to stir our sympathy for human relationship. This last is even more important than learning the geography of foreign lands.

—— Rabindranath Tagore: "A Poet's School", *Towards Universal Man*, Asia Publishing House, Bombay 1961. p. 300.

To allow freedom of thought and expression to the learners is to allow them to adjust and appreciate, and such an endeavour of adjustment and appreciation allows them to be more sensitive, creative and humane in their approach to learning. This is undeniably a socio-psychological adventure in education which demands a lot of dedication and devotion, sincerity and advancement. That man is always growing, always advancing is a definite proof of his inner growth the socio-aesthetic growth for which he must strive unendingly.

---

* Darwin makes a fine analysis of how man gradually develops himself in fourfold. Social urge to be aesthetically more distinct by means of instinctive, mental, aesthetic, and habitual changes. In his own words,

> .... Any animal whatever, endowed with well-marked social instincts, the parental and filial affections being here included, would inevitably acquire a moral sense or conscience, as soon as its intellectual powers had become as well, or nearly as well, developed as in man. For, *firstly*, the social instincts lead an animal to take pleasure in the society of its fellows, to feel a certain amount of sympathy with them, and to perform various services for them. The services may be of a definite and evidently instinctive nature; or there may be only a wish and readiness, as with most of the higher social animals, to aid their fellows in certain general ways. But these feelings and services are by no means extended to all the individuals in the same species, only to those of the same association. *Secondly*, as soon as the mental faculties had become highly developed, images of all past actions and motives would be incessantly passing through the brain of each individual;

> and that feeling of dissatisfaction, or even misery which invariably results from any unsatisfied instinct, would arise, as often as it was perceived that the enduring and always present social instinct had yielded to some other instinct, at the time stronger, but neither enduring in its nature, nor leaving behind it a very vivid impression. It is clear that many instinctive desires, such as that of hunger, are in their nature of short duration; and after being satisfied, are not readily or vividly recalled. *Thirdly*, after the power of language had been acquired, and the wishes of the community could be expressed, the common opinion how each member ought to act for the public good would naturally become in paramount degree the guide to action. But it should be borne in mind that, however great weight we may attribute to public opinion, our regard for the approbation and disapprobation of our fellows depends on sympathy, which, as we shall see, forms an essential part of the social instinct, and is indeed its foundation-stone. *Lastly*, habit in the individual would ultimately play a very important part in guiding the conduct of each member; for the social instinct, together with sympathy, is like any other instinct, greatly strengthened by habit, and so consequently would be obedience to the wishes and judgement of the community.

Charles R. Darwin: *The Descent of Man* , 1896. pp. 98-99

Tracing the history of man, Tagore points out how man has, by dint of socio-aesthetic refinement, been able touphold the true spirit of socialism and at the same time has been able to promote himself to a refined exponent of civilization. As he observes

Man loses his true stature when he fails to unite fully with his fellows. A complete man is one who has this capacity for union, a lone individual is a fragmented being.

* * * * * *

Let us examine on of the basic things when we say that man has really found himself by uniting with others. Man can speak, he has language. Through the unifying force of language a mind, otherwise sunk in itself, combines with others. It is through speech that the mind I have is projected into other minds, and those in turn become part of my own. This thinking in unison is an enrichment that negates inner poverty.

When mankind learnt to preserve language through the written word, the area of contact between minds was extended. Spoken words do not go far. They get lost in course of time, and often become distorted as they pass from mouth to mouth. But the written word crosses oceans and mountains and is still uncharged. Every man may thus gain the thinking of the countless others.

This is not all. The written word goes beyond uniting the minds of living men alone; it removes the barriers between the minds of today and the minds of those who belonged to a remote past. This great contact between thoughts has created what is called civilization. What is civilization but a state of union in which the strength of each individual adds power to all and the power of all fortifies the individual?

——— Rabindranath Tagore:"Co-operation",*Towards Universal Man*, Asia Publishing House, Bombay 1961. pp. 323-325.

That the strength of the individual is, indeed, the strength of the society and *vice-versa* , and that both individual and social development await a revolutionary approach to selfless service towards humanity have been further accentuated in Tagore's educational viewpoints on socio-aesthetic excellence. He places his spirit of idealism, the spirit of aesthetic fulfilment in terms of humble submission to truth whereby an individual plays his best part in the society. For this, Western marvels in science and technology, in literature and music, in fine arts and philanthropic activities necessitate a harmonizational approach to our own educational aims and objectives which, through a marriage of minds accidental and oriental pave newer avenues of socio-aesthetic furtherance in our country as well.

In the back-drop of the above viewpoints, Tagore places social development more on aesthetic and spiritual excellence than on material and scientific progress which prompt mankind towards greed and accumulation of wealth and prosperity. This is undeniably the avenue of leading a life in search of truth and joy as the ancient Indian civilization clearly proves in simple living and strenuous striving for a joyous and truth-conscious society. What Tagore said seventy years ago at a meeting of the teachers and students of Santiniketan on August 30, 1921 is even now relevant in the context of the modern global society bereft of cultivation of Truth and joy in day to day activities:

> Avarice is an evil passion, and for that reason it cannot create. Man's spiritual nexus is weakened when avarice becomes the motive power of a civilization. The greater the material wealth, strength and prosperity conferred by such a civilization, the less potent is the spiritual power of man.

A picture is not made of one line, but of the unity of many lines. All the lines long and short, are linked with one another, and their harmonized relation makes the picture. Plans for houses traced on blue wax-cloth are not to be called pictures; their lines are not related to one another by an inner, spiritual bond, but by an outer, practical need. A picture creates, a plan merely builds.

A society dominated by greedy commercialism becomes a huge plan with none of the qualities of a picture, and weakens the spiritual bonds between people. Wealth is the chariot of such a society, the wealthy man the charioteer; and the chariot is pulled by common folk harnessed to it by strong chains. As it rolls on with a clatter, civilization is said to progress. This triumphal march of the god of acquisitive wealth brings no joy to human beings since they have no real respect for such a god. When men are brought together merely by an outer bond, they rebel. This is clearly seen in the social revolution that has now overcast the European sky. Ancient India devitalized society by trying to unite people under the form, rather than the spirit, of religion and modern Europe is disrupting society by trying to unite them under social and economic, rather than moral and spiritual laws. Both those ways leave the human soul out of account and have little to do with spiritual truth.

** ** ** **

I have condemned the greed that is now enthroned in the heart of European civilizations. Why should greed be condemned? Because it does not lead to truth–so the *Isa Upanishad* answers. And to people who say that they

> do not care for truth, but only for enjoyment, the *Upanishad* answers, "Enjoy by all means. But then, there is no joy without truth". So the question now arises: "What is that truth?" It is the knowledge, the answer goes, that everything in this world is mantled over by God. Had the world been the ultimate truth, had there been nothing beyond the world, possession of earthly things would have been man's highest activity and greed his greatest source of gratification. But the highest truth is that God fulfils everything. It follows, therefore, that to experience that truth in the soul is man's highest activity.

Rabindranath Tagore: "The Unity of Education" *Towards Universal Man* Asia Publishing House, Bombay 1961. pp. 242-243.

To stick to truth for true socio-aesthetic manifestation of every individual should, as Tagore emphasizes, be the primary end in view of education and, for that, the liberation of an individual's soul awaits realization of the essence of truth within. This is also an experience in education-an experience that teaches universalism to forge ahead with the spirit of internationalism. The unity of education as he advocates is the unity of human minds in the society striving for the best efflorescence of Truth, Beauty and Goodness of mankind. He also goes further in spelling out education as a means for liberation and. expression of man's soul in unfolding the inner beauty of mankind—the beauty that perennially stands for socio-aesthetic poignance. And so, he hopes for such educational institution to be set up in India as would nurstle the culture of global socio-aesthetic excellence. In his own words,

> I hope that, on behalf of all countries of the East, India may soon found educational

> institutions where people from all parts of the world will meet for the pursuit of truth. Our country has the resources for doing this; it will be invited by evey country it invites, and will be treated as an honoured guest. But the question of honour or dishonour does not really arise. The essential thing is that truth should be realized within and expressed without, with the sole object of liberating and revealing man's soul. The doctrine of man's revelation must be propagated through our education, and practised through our action. Only then shall we be honoured by honouring all mankind, and shall overcome the infirmity of age by invoking a new age. He who sees all beings in his own self and his own self in all beings he does not remain unrevealed " that should be the motto of our Indian educational institutions.

Ibid . p. 251.

With the above socio-aesthetic viewpoints of being honoured by honouring mankind, Tagore actually invokes a new age of declaring his education mission which incorporates Nature as the ideal teacher of socio-aesthetic development of sensibilities side by side with freedom from all racial and national prejudice. His institution fosters 'the ideal of the spiritual unity of all races' where by the delicate sensibility of sympathy is nursled in the relentless endeavour of simplicity and creativity. In an article published in *The Modern Review* he exposes his viewpoints on setting up his institutions on the basis of this socio-aesthetic objective and invites the global people to join hands with him to fulfil his mission:

> Remembering the experience of my young days, of the school masters and the classrooms and also knowing something of the natural school which Nature herself supplies to all

her creatures, I established my institution in a beautiful spot far away from the town, where the children had the greatest freedom possible under the shade of ancient trees and the field around open to the verge of horizon.

From the beginning I tried to create an atmosphere which I considered to be more important than the class teaching. The atmosphere of nature's own beauty was there waiting for us from a time immemorial with her varied gifts of colours and dance, flowers and fruits, with the joy of her mornings and the peace of her starry nights.

From the commencement of our work we have encouraged our children to be of service to our neighbours from which has grown up a village reconstruction work in our neighbourhood, unique in the whole of India. Round our educational work the villages have grouped themselves in which the sympathy for nature and service for man have become one. In such extension of sympathy and service our mind realizes its true freedom.

Along with this has grown an aspiration for even a higher freedom, freedom from all racial and national prejudice. Children's sympathy is often deliberately made narrow and distorted making them incapable of understanding alien peoples with different languages and cultures. This causes us, when our growing souls demand it, to grope after each other in ignorance, to suffer from the blindness of this age. The worst fetters come when children lose their freedom of heart in love.

> We are building up our institution upon the ideal of the spiritual unity of all races. I hope it is going to be a great meeting place for individuals from all countries who believe in the divine humanity, and who wish to make atonement for the cruel disloyalty displayed against her by men.

> I represent in my institution an ideal of brotherhood, where man of different countries and different languages can come together. I believe in the spiritual unity of man and therefore I ask the world to accept this task from me.

—— Rabindranath Tagore: "My Educational Mission *The Modern Review* Calcutta, June 1931. pp. 621-623.

To feel the pulse of the global society right from childhood in an ideal natural atmosphere is to feel the inner pulse of mutual understanding and mutual respectability which undeniably contribute a great deal to the promotion and cultivation of socio-aesthetic poignance. To make children ideal citizens of future, who are quick to respond to nature and love, who are more interested in *being* than in *knowing* , who are truly sensitive to their relationship with the social atmosphere amidst joyous and vigorous activities, Tagore allows freedom of their all-round development in the social surroundings. Why does he allow freedom for development? Why does he give less importance to bare knowing? The answers are not far to seek. He values efflorescence of Truth amongst children more than anything else. He urges for 'union of perfect sympathy' in any endeavour at education for children's socialization in synchronization with development of aesthetic sensibilities. His own invaluable words on the above prove his socio-aesthetic mission:

> Freedom in the mere sense of independence is

meaningless. Perfect freedom lies in the harmony of relationship which we realize not through *knowing* but in *being*. Objects of knowledge maintain an infinite distance from us who are the knowers. For knowledge is not union. We attain the world of freedom only through perfect sympathy.

Children with the freshness of their senses come directly to the intimacy of this world. This is the first great gift they have. They must accept it naked and simple and never lose their power of quick communication. For our perfection we have to be at once savage and civilized; we must be natural with nature and human with human society.

I wish I could say that we have fulfilled this dream in our school. We have only made a beginning. We have given the children an opportunity to find their freedom in nature by being able to love it. For love is freedom; it saves us from paying with our soul for objects that are all too cheap. I know men who preach the cult of the simple life by glorifying the spiritual merit of poverty. I refuse to imagine any special value in poverty when it is a mere negation. Only when the mind is sensitive to the deeper call of reality is it weaned away from the lure of the fictitious. It is callousness which robs us of our simple power to enjoy and dooms us to the indignity of snobbish pride in furniture and the foolish burden of expensive things. But to pit the callousness of asceticism against the callousness of luxury is to fight one evil with another, inviting the pitiless demon of the desert in place of the indiscriminate demon of the jungle.

> With the help of literature, festive ceremonials and religious teachings I tried to develop in the children of my school their feeling for Nature as also a sensitiveness to their human surroundings. I prepared for them a real homecoming into this world. Among the subjects they learnt in the open air, in the shade of trees, were music and painting, and they had their dramatic performances.
>
> But this was not sufficient, and I waited for men and the means to be able to introduce into our school activities that would build up character. I felt the need of the western genius for imparting to my educational ideal the strength of reality which knew how to achieve a definite end of practical good.

—— Rabindranath Tagore: "A Poet's School", *Towards Universal Man*, Asia Publishing House Bombay. 1961. pp. 291-296.

To realize the fellowship of man and nature is to take the first lesson of socio-aesthetics. And for this, Tagore insists on realization of beauty and joy in the day-to-day life of man in the society. That the Goddess of Plenty is both beautiful and benign is to be learnt anew from man's association with Nature. Tracing the history of the socio-aesthetic harmony of mankind, Tagore shows how Earth-Mother endears man in the spirit of socio-aesthetic advancement. As he observes:

> In the primitive age men wandered alone, each in pursuit of their precarious livelihood. Their temper was fierce, their habits predatory; their behaviour unsocial. As, on river banks, food became plentiful, communities took form and civilizations were born.

Tilling the alluvial soil, men grew rich crops, year after year. They began to see that individuals could gain much more by mutual aid than by trying to deprive one another. With the food problem solved, the social instinct inherent in the nature of man was stimulated. When, at the invitation of the Earth-Mother, men sat down together, their isolated lives found a basis of brotherhood through their common food.

The realization came that in union there was not advantage alone but also satisfaction. For its sake the individual would accept suffering and even death. The Earth gives us food in such a way that it gladdens our eye and enraptures our mind. The golden sunlight flung from sky to sky, finds a response in the golden harvest from horizon to horizon. This splendour makes man think not only of his meals, but of festive rejoicings.

In the storehouse of the Earth there is, above the provision of our hunger, the nectar of joy. Lakshmi, the Goddess of Plenty, is beautiful as well as benign. The fruit tempts us not merely with its nutriment, but with its form, sweetness and fragrance. As the fruits of the Earth are beautiful, so also is the fellowship of man. The food we eat in solitude may have nourishment, but the food that we eat in fellowship has, in addition, loving-kindness. In such a feast of hearts the utensils become elegant, the serving decorous, the viands refined.

Dearth cramps the hospitality of man, on which society is founded. That is why villages had to grow on the threshold of the Earth's store of food. It was through his re-

> unions that the immortal in man has expressed itself; his morality, his literature, his music, his art, the variety of his ceremonials. It was through these that he began to be conscious of his own depths, and the ideal of his own perfection becomes manifest to him.

—— Rabindranath Tagore: "City and Village", *Towards Universal Man,* Asia Publishing House, Bombay. 1961. pp. 302-303.

To learn the lesson of socio-aesthetics from Nature and to cultivate it amongst the members of the society is the new dimension of education that Tagore strongly asserts for an enlightened global society. Such a society would allow every learner to appropriately exercise the power of inner vision and the mind, the skills of the body and its different parts, the devotion towards the birds and the beasts, the creepers and the trees, and the diverse elements of the universe. Moreover, there should be a decent experience of socio-aesthetic pattern of living together by keeping an eye to healthy habits of maintaining residence neat and clean, roads and houses trim and smart, dress, meal, bathing, exercise and rest balanced and proportioned, energetic and elegant. Let everyone be educated with the socio-aesthetic habits of hospitality and co-operation, service and devotion. Let each person honour the old and the infirm, children and aged persons, and above all, ideal mothers. Let there be a true harmonization of different castes and tribes. Let not the ego of creed take the upper hand over the mind and the society. Tagore as a socio-aesthetic thinker wants to disseminate that education which would eliminate the sense of ill-feeling or hatred towards any creed, custom, social functions and festr vals whatsoever, and pave the wider avenues of manifestation of Beauty, Goodness and Truth to enable everyone to be truly social.

Looking upon man as an embodiment of inner socio-aesthetic force, Tagore never allows man to be dwarfed by a stronger force. Nor does he allow society or for that end in view civilization to be dwarfed by allowance of charity. He wants to raise the inner indomitable power of man to utilize his socio-aesthetic vision for the welfare of one and all. Education, therefore, is a process of understanding and appreciating the human rights that can bring about true social and aesthetic development in making*. As a practical socio-aesthetic reformer, Tagore beckons for a concerted endeavour to revitalize the rural society with the socio-aesthetic spirit of love and patience, amity and perserverance. To undertake such a challenging task, he believes that the youth in the societv are the fittest persons to bring out desirable changes among rural people. His own words of

* That Tagore is instrumental in bringing about a revolutionary concept of social development among the masses has been finely delineated as a new challenge as follows :

> He [Tagore] had always felt for them, pitied them and taken the upper classes to task for neglecting their duties towards them. Indeed, he had even tried to bring his own share of contribution to improve the lot of the underdogs in society. But never having questioned the basic social arrangement, he had found no satisfactory solution for their problems, true to his own inner development, however, he began to recognise the fact that no permanent good could be done to them by mere charity.

> "But the trouble is", the poet significantly remarks, "that nothing permanent can be built up on charity; to try to do good from without is vitiated at every step. Only from equals can one expect real help. I have not been able to think it all one satisfactorily, but to assume that progress can be maintained only by

keeping down the bulk of humanity and denying them their human rights is a reapproach to the mind.

"Man cannot do good to those whom he does not respect. No sooner is one's self-interest at stake than a clash arises. Radical solution of this problem is being sought in Russia. *(Russiar Chithi).*

... Tagore's interest in economic problems arose primarily from his own early experiences. When through the accident of family circumstances he first came into contact with the rural population, the old village economy still retained its traditional character. The age-old dichotomy of India's political and social organistion was thus borne in upon him through personal knowledge. As he says:

... Where the responsibility for the welfare of the people lies, there beats the heart of the nation and if a blow should fall thereon, the whole nation is wounded unto death. In England the overthrow of the State would mean the destruction of the nation. But disaster can only overatake our country when its social body, its *Samaj*, is crippled. That is why we never staked our all to resist a change of sovereignty, but clung with might and main to the freedom of our *Samaj*, *("Swadeshi Samaj", Greater India)*.

—— Sasadhar Sinha: "The New Challenge", *Social Thinking of Rabindranath Tagore*, Asia Publishing House, Bombay. 1962. pp. 12-13.

---

advice to the young reveals how he nurses in his own mind the most thrilling and concerete ideas on rural reconstruction along socio-aesthetic dimension:

> Whosoever and wheresoever amongst you are able, take the responsibility of a village each and have shelter there. Arrange the villages. Impart education on agriculture and industry, introduce new endeavour about rural matters of daily use. Infuse that enthusiasm amongst them, which might lead to cleanliness, of the rural people's residence and which allow beauty and healthfulness. Innovate that principle which might inspire them to assemble together and execute all the activities of the village. Do not expect fame for this work; even, instead of having gratitude from the villagers, constraints and disbelief would have to be admitted. There is no excitement in it, nor is there any opposition or declaration. Only patience and love, meditation in silence -- a single promise in the mind that, we would submit the whole life to alleviate the sorrows, at their roots, of the sorrowful people of the country by sharing their sorrows.

—— Rabindranath Tagore: "*Atmasakti O Samuha*", *Rabindra Rachanavali*, Government of West Bengal, Calcutta. Tagore Birth Centenary Edition. 1961 Vol. XII. pp. 824-825.

[Translated by me.

The beckoning for a united endeavour to mitigate the social woes and discrepancics as Tagore makes, is not a sentimental or romantic flight of imagination as most social workers are even now prone to do so to fulfil narrow interests, but a genuine urge to contribute as much as posisble to revive and enrich everyone's social and aesthetic poignance inherent in him. As a matter of fact, he strongly intends to do away with social misunderstandings and bring about a sense of harmony and concerted endeavour to achieve a serene socio-aesthetic pattern of living everywhere. True to this above principle, he suggests in theory the following prin—

ciples for organising the different activities of the country:

> First, unless we make a synchronization between the nature of the present time and the condition of our country, we would have to face extinction. The nature of the present time is; alignment, defence, organisation. In spite of having all the noble qualities, nothing would survive today against unionism by any means. Therefore, the separatism, the signs of death that are observed in every village amongst us, would have to be given a check by arranging the villages in no time.
>
> Second our consciousness is not reaching every part of the nation. And so all our efforts have been nourished at some places and ematiated elsewhere. As differences are being crept up in different ways between the masses and the intelligentsia, the sense of unity of the nation is not being translated into reality.
>
> Third, this sense of unity cannot by any means, be translated into reality by mere advice or discussion. If the intelligentsia disseminate their endeavour of activities among the masses, then alone the union of our hearts would automatically be infused uninterrupted.

Ibid . P. 825

The passivity born of disappointments among the masses in the society is in most cases due to increasing differences between the enlightened and the ignorant, between the adored and the despised. Tagore strikes at the root of these appalling differences in the society when man has lost faith in man and is undergoing severe stress and strain both mentally and physically. The finer sensibilities of life are dwarfed by such apathy and differences which have allowed many antagonistic camps with different ideologies in the rural society. The sufferings of humanity pave the moratorium of aesthetics. Belief has already become an alien word with class--consciousness and class--hatred. Tagore rightly cautions humanity against the perils of passivity and hopelessness, which demand a greater sacrifice and a nobler ideal of socio-aesthetic excellence.

To awaken the inner socio-aesthetic sensibilities in every person in the society, Tagore advises us not to be disheartened with our little bit of abilities, nor to be disappointed with our little bit of strength but to be positive in our approach to the well-being of the society. Even when the country was under the British yoke and was ruthlessly oppressed both mentally and physically in any endeavour at making any positive approach to bring about socio-aesthetic change in the country, his advice is not to dole out good sense and sensibilities but to arrest all sorts of haughtiness of mind, of sentimentalism or emotionalism so that every one in the society might ardently contribute to the progress of the country. This alone will show how everyone can, through calm and cool attitude to social activities, bring about significant social welfare not for the time being but permanently. What, therefore, is essentially required for launching any constructive social work is primarily to arouse and activate the inner spirit of socio-aesthetics so that there is no room for littleness in any social endeavour whatsoever. Not hatred but goodwill and love, not ill or misbehaviour but calmness of mind and patience every time and everwhere are some of the fundamental attitudes towards which our attention should be by all means directed. While explaining the key to success as a true social emancipator, he has the following words to be seriously pondered over:

> The habit of giving a reply, of outwitting in turn moves us away from real work and

success. When a man is about to file a suit in arrogance, he does not even hesitate to bring about his own ruin. Likewise, if we continually try to make ourselves angry by patting the heated words of mental disappointments, then the objectives of having the desirable ends in view recede far and far away and the satisfaction of anger takes the upper hand. In order to keep an observation towards the appropriate and intensive good of the country, one should emancipate oneself from the clutches of petty temptation. If one keeps oneself agitated and irritated the sense of weightage in every affair withers away--a little matter becomes a legion-one's poignance is jeopardised by uncontrolled extravagance by taking recourse to every littleness. With such frivolousness, weakness alone is increased. It cannot be called as organisation of strength; it is a wailing of inabilities.

—— Rabindranath Tagore: "*Atmasakti O Samuha Rabindra Rachanavali*, Government of West Bengal, Calcutta. Tagore Birth Centenary Edition. 1961 Vol. XII. pp. 719-720.

[Translated by me.

To launch an effective programme of social activities, Tagore specially emphasizes on a sound mind that never allows any sort of littleness or dwarfness. It does not also allow ill-planned, extravagant activities to be executed parasitically. What is greatly needed as a socio-aesthetic worker for the well-being of the country is to uphold the spirit of love in every action and upon every person in the society. As a matter of fact, to establish the good of the country is to nurture and establish love in the heart of every countryman, win his confidence and entrust him to perform whatever he can for the well-being of the country. Feebleness here has no room, for this alone eats up the aesthetic vitalities of one's devotion to service towards the society, nor is there any room for hatred and arrogance because these are enough to destroy the sincere course of any socio-aesthetic action. One should have to exercise ones own creative endeavour to liberate oneself from the darkness of ignorance and apathy. One should, at the same time, identify the different manifestations of evil propensities that one normally comes across in course of any socio-aesthetic operation. This will enable one to liberate oneself from sentimentalism and passivity by dint of rigorousness in action through strict but loving maintenance of discipline and control and restraint in behaviour. Let no action social, aesthetic or whatsoever, be messed up with the darkness of sentimentalism or arrogance.

Tagore has exended his vision of socio-humanism mainly at par with the above viewpoints of socio-aesthetics. Time and again he refers to the vision of a greater India born of her rich socio-cultural and socio-humanistic heritage which defies religious and other differences to promote better personal and social relationship. This also indicates how Tagore refers to the greater truth of socio-aesthetics which teaches us the lesson of how to identify and exercise the common and unchanging basis of global unity of mankind, to endear every member of the society as our very own and to establish a greater bond of socio-aesthetic relationship among mankind. He, therefore, urges on revitalising our socio-aesthetic viewpoints of global humanism by going back to the source-point of the real wealth of India:

> The real wealth of India was never hidden like an old legal document in an iron safe. The only true expression of India was in that which she gave openly and freely. The surplus of her cultural life, which she scattered everywhere, was the care of her personality. Through the capacity to give we earn the right to call the outsider our own, and transcend the barriers of geography. So if we want to know

what the true wealth of India consisted of, we should have to cross watery barriers to reach the far-off fields of her self-dedication. From India abroad we may glimpse that enternal grace we often fail to grasp, enveloped as we are by the dust storm of modern history.

Even our mediaeval history bears witness to this. In our Middle Ages there was a religious conflict between the Hindus and the conquering Muslims. But during that time we also find a succession of saints and devotees -- many Muslims among that galaxy – who bridged the gulf of religious differences of personal relationship. They were not politicians and could not even dream of accepting as a reality the so called political union which was based on opportunism. They went where mankind finds its common and unchanging basis of unity, and they accepted, as their motto, the great truth which teaches us to see *all* as part of ourselves. There were in those days many heroes whose names have been recorded in our history books based on foreign models, but they are now lost amidst the dustheap which summarizes their glory. But the deathless message of those saints and devotees are still running in the life-stream of the Indian people. If we could draw our inspiration from that source, we would see an improvement in our politics and economics and also strengthening in our global plan of action.

Rabindranath Tagore: "Greater India", Quoted from *Rabindranath Tagore* by Sisir Kumar Ghosh, Sahitya Academy, New Delhi, 1986. pp. 126-127.

Remaining faithful to the above socio-aesthetic and socio-humanistic viewpoints, Tagore himself launches an experiment in his own institution of national and international repute -- Visva Bharati -- to promote good will between the nations and races of mankind. Accordingly, he unfolds the socio-aesthetic vision of India in terms of her rich socio-cultural and socio-aesthetic heritage, her relationship with Asia and her kinship with the global society. As Marjorie Sykes characteristically notes.

> The work of Visva-Bharati can be thought of as growing up in three concentric circles. The innermost circle is the circle of India. Rabindranath, the patriot, wanted Indians to learn to understand and love all the treasures of their own country. The social traditions, literature, art, music of India contain rich treasures which vary from place to place. Rabindranath saw clearly that it was not enough to know only one's own province, language or religion. He himself loved Bengal deeply, but he never forgot that Bengal is only part of India. It is good that love should be deep, but it must not be narrow. It is right that a Muslim should feel proud of the greatness of Islam, that a Bengali should be proud of his musical language, and that a Tamil should be proud of the saints and poets of Tamil Nad. But, said Rabindranath, this good and rightful pride will become a false and poisonous one if we do not respect and honour different forms of greatness in other provinces, languages and creeds. Visva-Bharti, therefore, welcomes students from every part of India. They live together in the same hostels and eat in the same dining room. In the Music School, the Manipuri dance from Assam is taught side by side with the Kathakali from Travancore. Students learn to appreciate and understand Rabindranath's modern Bengali music and at the same time to take an interest in

the traditional schools. The art school has in its museum treasures from every part of India--paintings, carvings, pottery, embroideries--which are placed in turn, one by one, in a special case in the centre of the *ashram* where everyone can see and enjoy them.

* * * * *

The second circle is the circle of Asia, Persia and India, Ceylon, Burma and Malaya, Tibet, China and Japan, are all parts of one great continent. Travellers, traders and teachers have journeyed to and fro across this continent for thousands of years. China and India are the homes of civilizations which are thousands of years old. The teaching of Gautama Buddha was first given in India but it has spread more widely still. . . .

From time to time, students from all these lands have been enrolled in one or other department of Visva-Bharati. In this way the students are helped to realise that no country is ever completely independent of other countries in its thought or art of civilization. . . .

The third circle is the world circle which includes along with Asia the civilization of the West, of Europe and America. Every invader of Indian history, from the Aryans onwards, has contribued something of value to the rich civilization of the country. Rabindranath believed that the British also, the latest comers, have valuable contribution to make. India must not turn her back on Western culture, but study and understand it, and learn the lessons it can teach her.

—Marjorie Sykes: *Rabindranath Tagore*, Longmans. pp. 85-89.

Not conservatism but a wider dissemination of global socio-aesthetics is the inner vision of Rabindranath Tagore as an unparalleled exponent of socio-aesthetic synchronizer. Admittedly, where he departs from other socio-political thinkers is that a real worth while social change is possible only when there is a concerted endeavour to bring about mass consciousness through popular media available in our country like the *melas* and the *jatras* which are not only vehicles of mass enjoyment but also exposers of inner socio-aesthetic vision enriched in age-old tradition of the country. Education, then, deserves arousal of this great inner socio-aesthetic spirit of our countrymen who are even now swept more by the whirling wind of sham political sentimentalism than by a genuine urge for socio-aesthetic revolution*. Tagore's own exposition on man's relation to man as social being serves as an invaluable reminder for nurturing of socio-aesthetic consciousness:

> To establish the bond of kinship between man and man was the most fundamental endeavour of India. This kinship would have to be maintained with distant relatives, relationship with sons, though aged, would not be loosened, appropriate and due bonds of relationship would have to be maintained with the rural people irrespective of caste and position. There is an appropriate bond of relationship always maintained with everyone between the master and the priest, the guest and the beggar, the landlord and the tenants or the servants. These are not merely.

---

*The essence of his teaching was two fold. Politically he brought a new seriousness to bear on the national movement which was previously altogether lacking. For the first time, he demonstrated the need to view India's struggle for freedom primarily in the social context. It was, he thought, neither a question of constitutional changes nor of ridding the country of foreign rule. The problem was deeper. It was, in fact, a question of finding a new basis of social integration which had been destroyed by the impact of industrial civilisation of the West. The social implications of India's political slavery were clearly brought out in the essays he wrote in this period and he showed the way to a fresh approach to the country's economic and political problems. In a real sense, therefore, this may be called the beginning of the constructive phase in India's national struggle. By stressing the paramount need for the rehabilitation of the rural economy of India, he not only gave proof of his historical acumen, but also helped to bring into relief the crucial importance of one aspect of India's social structure which held the key to the solution of the country's future. In analysing the causes of India's mass poverty, Tagore showed the true genius of his mind, and subsequent happenings revealed the correctness of his social diagnosis. He warned his countrymen from the very beginning against relying too much on constitutional agitation for the achievement of freedom from foreign domination. His insistence on mass contact, the need for co-operative activities for the solution of India's grave economic problems, the utilisation of traditional rural institiitions like *melas* and *jatras* for the rousing of popular consciousness and mass enjoyment were at one time looked at askance by his follow countrymen, but in the light of later developments Tagore was proved right. Thanks to Mahatma Gandhi's leadership, the whole emphasis of politics in India has shifted from the towns to the villages where the bulk of the country's populations live. The originality of the poet's political thinking, however, has not yet received adequate recognition, but in retrospect his claim to this honour rests on solid foundations.

The poet's interest in education, as has been seen, was always more than academic. He had already taken a hand in the moulding of the country's eduational theories by his notable experiment at Santiniketan. In its genesis it was, of course, an individualistic attempt to grapple with a personal problem, but the *Swadeshi* movement was soon to drag Tagore to wider fields of educational activity. From his own experience as an educationist, the poet has seen the limitations of a purely personal approach to education and was looking for an opportunity to broaden its scope so as to embrace the whole nation. He realised that the human child abstracted from his social background must always remain ill-adopted to his surroundings. The leading part that he took in formulating national ideals of education in the formative period of the nation's history was unique for many reasons. He never took a narrow view of the country's educational problems. He deprecated the idea of multiplying schools which were national merely in name but were in no other way different from the existing schools. He looked upon education as a vehicle of national progress and wanted it to be based on the real needs of the country in the same way as education is conceived in the advanced countries of the world. Unfortunately, however, the other leaders thought differently, and the national school movement, in spite of its seminal possibilities, came to nothing.

—— Sasadhar Sinha: *Social Thinking of Rabindranath Tagore*, Asia Publishing House, Bombay. 1962 pp. 138-139.

> Moral relations as ordained by the scriptures but also a relationship of the heart. Some of them either hold the position of a father or of a son, a brother or of an aged. Whenever we come in contact with any person, we ascertain some sort of relationship with him. For this, we cannot, under any circumstances, think man as an instrument of performing our activities; nor can we think him as a part of the machine.

Rabindranath Tagore: "*Atmasakti O Samuha*", *Rabindra Rachanavali*, Government of West Bengal, Calcutta, Tagore Birth Centenary Edition. 1962. Vol. XII. p. 690.

[Translated by me

The image of man as a socio-aesthetic promoter of mankind that Tagore visualizes and translates into reality in his own experimentations at Sriniketan and Santiniketan is yet to be adored as a pointer to socio-aesthetic advancement in our heavily bruised and affluence-arrested society. The voice of loneliness in the crowded society of carelessness is never lost. Nor can the agonies of the schizophrenic society awaiting the doomsday of man be silenced by sheer affluence. Almost ostracized, by oursleves even in our hearts, we cannot but sing the song of prayer to be reenkindled for the blemishes of the little soul *sans* the blessings of the society or the All Serene:

> I came out alone on my way to my tryst.
> But who is this that follows me in the silent dark?
> I move aside to avoid his presence
> but I escape him not.

He makes the dust rise from the earth
with his swagger; he adds his loud voice
to every word that I utter.
He is my own little self, my lord, he
knows no shame; but I am ashamed to come to
thy door in his company.

—— Rabindranath Tagore: "*Gitanjali*", Macmillan India Limited, New Delhi. Macmillan Pocket Tagore Edition, 1981. No. XXX. pp. 17-18.

Are we prepared to sing?

4

EDUCATION FOR PROMOTION OF SOCIAL COHESION

TAGOREAN PERSPECTIVES

Education is always a process of promotion of individual excellence from manifold dimensions. It spurts one's consciousness and enkindles one to be what one should be in relation to others. Bereft of others, one loses one's real identity. Education, indeed, is one's endeavour — continual and, therefore, ceaseless—to foster this identity in the best possible manner. Hence, socialization of man. For an individual to be an individual in the most natural and desirable end in view, the social avenues of individual efflorescence necessitate appropriate exploration, expansion, nursling and adoration. How can an individual explore the best possible avenues of efflorescence of his sociabilities? How can he expand the horizon of social cohesion? What are the invaluable components contributing unendingly to nursling and appreciation of desirable socialization? These and a host of numerous other queries come under the domain of worthwhile efflorescence of individuality.

Deeply shocked at the appalling signs of littleness of individuality and social disintegration, Rabindranath Tagore wages a war against the marooned individual already purchased with the coins of utilitarianism and abstraction. At the same time, he points out the wounds of the indigenous society heavily inflicted by the colonial infiltration to imitate alien social culture and tradition on the one hand and nourish class-distinction and class-hatred on the other. The clerk-oriented education thrivingly supplemented by the alien yoke has allowed to breed the almost indestructible germs of the advantaged and the disadvantaged in the society: the differences between the haves and the have-nots writ large even now in our society in a more or less stabilised manner, and what is more unfortunate is that even now education has not been given its proper platform to play the most vital role of social and national cohesion. Significantly enough, Tagore has drawn our attention towards education for individual excellence to promote social cohesion. The social imbalances owing to aimlessness in education deeply pains him and so he earnestly appeals to be optimistic in our approach to society, to have clarity of vision by means of acquiring consistency of power of vision for a reorganised and thriving society. In elucidating the role of education to foster the spirit of an optimistic society, he remarks :

> We have no clarity in our life. Nowhere in our country is there any specific indication of what we can be or how far we can aspire. The authority to desire makes the power of man forceful. In the caressing of Nature there cannot be any wastage of energy. For this, where there is no hope, force bids farewell from there. In

> science it is said that when sighted animals live for long in cages, they lose vision. As nature cannot tolerate the inconsistency of power of vision in the absence of light, so it is unbearable for her to have power *sans* hope. For this when there is no way out but to flee away in the face of danger, the power to run away also becomes arrested.

Rabindranath Tagore: "*Lakshya O Siksha*" ("Aims and Education"), *Siksha*, Visva-Bharati, Santiniketan, 1973. p. 130

[Translated by me

'To know man and to make oneself known to man as Tagore categorically asserts is the prime objective of education which brings man nearer to man. Such an education is more than mere intellectual pursuit or a passport to bare livelihood but a real sharing of knowledge and experiences, art and culture, creativity and mutual consciousness in an ever expanding global society. Can man remain deaf to the eternal voice of man awaiting a genuine social revolution? How far is education geared to that end in view? How far is it related to socio-aesthetic and socio-spiritual coherence of man? These are some of the questions which should essentially initiate everyone interested in education for social cohesion. Accordingly, Tagore in his treatise entitled "An Eastern University" dwells upon this very social foundation of education and humanism:

> The great use of Education is not merely to collect facts, but to know man and to make oneself known to man. It is the duty of every human being to master, at least to some extent, not only the language of intellect, but also that personality which is the language of Art. It is a great world of reality for man, — vast and profound, — this growing world of his own crea-

tive nature. This is the world of Art. To be brought up in ignorance of it is to be deprived of
tive nature. This is the world of Art. To be brought up in ignorance of it is to be deprived of the knowledge and use of that great inheritance of humanity, which has been growing and waiting for every one of us from the beginning of our history. It is to remain deaf to the eternal voice of Man, that speaks to all men the messages that are beyond speech. From the educational point of view we know Europe where it is scientific, or at best literary. So our notion of its modern culture is limited within the boundary lines of grammar and the laboratory. We almost complete ignore the aesthetic life of man, leaving it uncultivated, allowed weeds to grow there. Our newspapers are prolific, our meeting places are vociferous; and in them we wear to shreds the things we have borrowed from our English teachers. We make the air dismal and damp with the tears of our grievances. But where are our arts, which, like the outbreak of spring flowers, are the spontaneous overflow of our deeper nature and spiritual magnificence ?

Through this great deficiency of our modern education, we are condemned to carry to the end a dead load of dumb wisdom. Like miserable outcasts, we are deprived of our place in the festival of culture, and wait at the outer court, where the colours are not for us, nor the forms of delight, nor the songs. Ours is the education of a prison-house, with hard labour and with a drab dress cut to the limits of minimum decency and necessity. We are made to forget that the perfection of colour and form and expression belongs to the perfection vitality,— that the joy of life is only the other side of

> the strength of life. The timber merchant may think that the flowers and foliage are mere frivolous decorations of a tree; but if these are suppressed, he will know to his cost that the timber too will fail.

—— Rabindranath Tagore: "An Eastern University", *Creative Unity, Macmillan & Co., Limited*, London, 1962. p 196-198.

Keeping in view the above invaluable words of creative and aesthetic socialization of man as Tagore delineates, it is undeniable that these words are yet to serve as forethoughts for our onward march for social integration. Adoration of sham culture, devaluation of art and aesthetic sensibilities that are in vogue in our society from time immemorial, derecognition of values prevalent in the society and dissipation towards tolerance and sympathy are some of the dangerous symptoms that are gradually eating up the vitalities of coherence of a diversified and conglomerative society. When Tagore speaks on the real aims and objectives of education, he warns against such vicissitudes in education as would isolate man from man in the society. Rather would it expand the horizon of education so that by dint of inquisitiveness and dynamism through education, man might find out the most appropriate avenue of the welfare of the society. Let the society be integrated in the true sense of the term and let education remove all ill thoughts of failure or hopelessness of the masses of the society. Let the manifold powers and resources of every one in the society be properly identified and utilized for social prosperity. In his words,

> If the sphere of hope becomes great, the power of mankind also becomes great and thrives. The power then gets its power to visualize its avenues distinctly and forcefully steps on. Any society that can afford the greatest thing to mankind is the greatest hope. It is not everyone in the society achieves complete suc-

> cess of that aspiration. But as there is always an inclination towards that hope directly or indirectly, **everyone's power can proceed till its** end. It is the most important thing for a nation. There is no value of population; but power and resources whatsoever of most of the people of the society are being utilized and are not buried in the ground —that is called prosperity. Where power is dynamic, goodness prevails there. Where wealth becomes living and are being utilized, therein lies grandeur.

—— Rabindranath Tagore: "*Lakshya O Siksha* ", ("Aims and Education") *Siksha,* Visva-Bharati, Santiniketan, 1973, pp. 130-131.

[Translated by me.

For a real atmosphere of social cohesion, education as Tagore earnestly feels must bring forth the social sense of oneness, the feeling for one and all. Then alone a living relationship between man and man in the society would be established in the most ideal and natural manner. He also strongly emphasises on the awareness of truth and hospitality which are nothing but outcomes of education for sharing social responsibilities amply contributing to worthwhile democracy. As he significantly remarks,

> A living relationship in a physical, or in a social body depends upon sympathetic collaboration and helpfulness between the various individual organs or members. When a perfect balance of interchange begins to operate, a consciousness of unity develops that is no longer easy to obstruct. The resulting health or wealth are both secondary to this sense of unity which is the ultimate end and aim, and a creation in its own right. Whenever some sectarian

> ambition for power establishes a dominating position in life's republic, the sense of unity, which can only be generated and maintained by a perfect rhythm of reciprocity between the parts, is bound to be disturbed. In a society where the greed of an individual or of a group is allowed to grow uncontrolled, and is encouraged or even applauded by the populace, democracy, as it is termed in the West, cannot be truly realised. In such an atmosphere a constant struggle goes on among individual to capture public organisations for the satisfaction of their own personal ambition. Thus democracy becomes like an elephant whose one purpose of life is to give joy rides to the clever and to the rich. The organs of information and expression, through which opinions are manufactured, and the machinery of administration are openly or secretly manipulated by the prosperous few, by those who have been compared to the camel which can never pass through the needle's eye, that narrow gate that leads to the kingdom of ideals. Such a society necessarily becomes inhospitable, suspicious, and callous towards those who preach their faith in ideals, in spiritual freedom. In such a society people becomes intoxicated by the constant stimulation of what they are told as progress, like the man for whom wine has greater attraction than food.

—— Rabindranath Tagore: Presidential Address under the auspices of the Visva-Bharti Sammilan at the Rammohan Library, Calcutta, July 28, 1922 published as "Introduction to the Robbery of the Soul' in L.K. Elmhirst: *Poet and Ploughman*, Visva-Bharti, Calcutta. 1975. Pp. 35.

To make room for healthy social cohesion by means

of education is as Tagore time and again makes us aware, to do away with social superstitions. This is the only radical approach to bring about dynamism in educational advancement. Learning, then, will be based on truth and 'the robbery of the soul' committed by social prejudices will be successfully arrested. How will it be arrested? What are the social components to be revived through education? Tagore has very definite answer. It is to arouse and cultivate the serene sense of reverence between the teacher and taught between man and man in society and remove all barriers of manifestation of truth in every direction. As he poignantly observes,

> Change of social conditions are continually taking place and would continually take place; nobody can check it, but if all arrangements are made permanent, nothing can be more distressing to the human being. How is it? Just as river is receding but the permanent steps of the river remain as they were; the way for the ferry service boat remains fixed at the same place: if anyone disembarks elsewhere than that point he is ostracised. There are, therefore, points of arrival and departure, but no service is possible.
>
> Under such circumstances, our society does not impart us education in keeping with our time. It is providing us with the education of two or four thousand, years ago. Therefore, the school to build up as man and greater than any other institution is closed to us. It has no claim towards leading the life at par with the present era. Once, under certain special circumstances of our history, our society dictated men to be Brahmins, Kshatriyas, Vaishyas and Sudras as necessary. It has a claim towards us in accordance with the appropriateness of time. Therefore, keeping an eye to this claim the system of

> education was creating itself out of its own in diverse forms. This *is* the rule of creation. A seed of the original idea thrives with its own branches in a natural way out of the demands of life, nobody attaches from outside branches to it. In our present day society there is no living claim. Even now it is speaking to man, 'Be a Brahmin, be a Sudra'. It is not possible by any means to truly carry out whatever it is speaking and as such man is accepting all this from outside.

—— Rabindranath Tagore: *"Sikshavaidhi"* ("Principles of Education") *Siksha*, Visva-Bharti, 1973 pp. 125-126.

[Translated by me.

Tagore also enhances the importance of bringing forth a certain aesthetic sense of respect in the process of education to highlight social enrichment and social cohesion He firmly believes that unless their is an aesthetic bond of relationship between man and society, the purpose of education cannot but be jeopardised. This is certainly an indication of loss of faith with which the modern society is badly afflicted and education remains a passive onlooker to all forms of sham behavioural manifestations in society A society which allows hypocrisy to reign supreme shows its back to all high-sounding objectives of education for advancement of social harmony, and the sense of doing good to the members of the society is replaced by miseducation that remains passive and exercises histrionics in everchanging behavioural patterns. What Tagore spoke nearly eighty years ago about the sorry state of affairs in education in relation to society awaits sincere attention even now:

> We are paying the price and accepting it but in exchange to that no truth emerges. The disciple finishes his duty by saluting the master

as honorarium, but the master is not even making an endeavour to allow the disciple to repay the debt, and in the forgotten language of ancient times, the master is delivering sermon to the disciple. The disciple has neither respect, nor ability nor intentions to accept that. Consequently, we are gradually losing the belief that there is a necessity of whatever is true. We do not even feel shame to the least extent to admit that it is enough if we maintain external demeanour. We do not even hesitate to say: 'Do whatever you will in practice, but if you don't admit it publicly, there is no harm in it.' Man is to take recourse to such type of falsehood under pressure. This is because, when your reverence has taken different direction, then, if the society keeps the custom close to the same place by dint of rigorous administration, the maximum member of people in the society do not feel it a shame to take recourse to falsehood. This is because, among men, the number of heroes is few. Therefore, where the punishment for explicitly divulging the truth is unbearingly high, hypocrisy can no longer be considered to be a crime there. For this, a peculiar matter is observed everyday in our country: Man accepts a thing to be good at ease at one time, but at that very moment he can unhesitatingly say; I shall not be able to carry it out for social use.' We also **excuse this *sham* behavioural pattern thinking** how impossibly high the price is to work out one's belief of truth in action in this society.

—— *Ibid* . pp. 126-127
Translated by me.

That the difference between human action and contemplation is rapidly changing its course by means of continual increase in social disintegration and that education is yet to bring about a purposeful, effective and lasting change in social awareness can hardly be overestimated. In fact, where social discrepancies appear either in the form of social taboos or in social superstitions education is yet to uproot the social evils on a war footing. And for such an action a band of devoted teachers in the practical social arena might revolutionize the whole society to be worthy of upholding the true spirit of nationalism. Education for acceleration of social harmony, therefore, greatly necessitates a band of teachers who are well-prepared to sacrifice their own interests to provide pupils with the spirit of dynamism to know the people of the country first, and all their efforts at advancement of learning should be geared to liberate the mind to go ahead to discover the thrilling avenues of universal brotherhood of man. Mere political awakening or class-consciousness in the name of social synchronization would serve very little purpose. Even when we talk about national education today it should be recrystallized in terms of Tagore's wider approach to education as a dynamic and all-embracing process of human development. As he poignantly suggests,

> If we can activate the currents of education in our country by means of manifold experiments of different teachers, then alone it would be a natural phenomenon of our country. Then alone we would come across real teachers at different places and at different times. Then, the generation of teachers would obviously thrive on. We cannot innovate a special principle of education by stamping it as a 'national' one. The multidimensional endeavour of indigenous persons can be termed as 'national'. What with indigenous or with foreign rule, when a particular principle of education wants to entangle the whole country with a fired ideal, we would not be able to christen it as national'. It is communal and, therefore, very

dangerous for a nation.

—*Ibid* . p. 128.

[Translated by me.

How can education play vital role for emergence of true national and social cohesion? Who plays the most significant role in education? According to Tagore, it is the teacher who alone serves as the touchstone of true social revolution and social cohesion. His own way of leading the life serves as a living example for the pupils who are enkindled with the serene vision of education to bring forth inward revolution—the effulgence of humanism. And so, the first lesson starts with an intense, pulsating, serene relationship between the teacher and the taught-a relationship about which Tagore writes:

Like the current of blood in a living body educational activities can continue through total relationship between the teacher and the taught. This is because the responsibilities of child-rearing and teaching the child actually rest on parents. But as parents are wanting in that eligibility or advantage, the assistance of other appropriate persons become mandatory. Under such circumstances the teachers cannot but be parents. We cannot purchase the best thing of life nor can we partly accept it. With affection, love, and devotion alone can we make it our own. That alone is the enzyme of the digestive system of humanity; that alone can unite living materials with life. At present, in the education of our country, that very life of the teacher has become very necessary. There is nothing more formidable than lifeless education in early life. It crushes out and extracts more than what it imparts the mind. In our social system we are seeking that teachers who would liberate the course of movement of our mind. By any means whatsoever, we want man in every direction. In its stead, no physician would be able to safeguard us by stifling the pills of strategies.

—*Ibid* . p. 129.

[Translated by me.

For the efflorescence of humanism in our system of education, what, then, is of absolute importance is to have a radical approach to social cohesion which has a paramount role in education for dynamism. Any ideal for organisation of nation and, for that end in view social cohesion rests on successful manifestation of the living spirit of the people who freely and spontaneously exercise their unique power of creative and critical thinking in their onward march for better social cohesion and solidarity. Admittedly, monotony in education and human behaviour leads to dwarfing the power of an individual's self-expression. A foreseer of global social cohesion, Tagore warns against the appalling limitations of nation. A nation *sans* its creative and socio-creative clienteles is no nation as it simply toys with production and destruction just as computerised nation of today does. The history of man is in doldrums not because the nations are prone to professionalism alone but also because the harmony of conjoint communicated social life is lost in the melee of sham nationalism where education is yet to play its significant role to liberate it from hatred, greed, jealousy and numerous other destructive components which make man the greatest enemy of man. As Tagore strongly asserts:

> In the modern world the fight is going on between the living spirit of the people and the methods of nation-organising. It is like the struggle that began in central Asia between cultivated areas of man's habitation and the continually encroaching desert sands, till the human region of life and beauty was choked out of existence. When the spread of higher ideals of humanity is not held to be important, the hardening method of national efficiency

gains a certain strength; and for some limited period of time, at least, it proudly asserts itself as the fittest to survive. But it is the survival of that part of man which is the least living. And this is the reason why dead monotony is the sign of the spread of the Nation. The modern towns, which present the physiognomy due to this dominance of the Nation, are everywhere the same, from San Francisco to London, from London to Tokyo. They show no faces, but merely masks.

The peoples, being living personalities, must have their self-expression, and this leads to their distinctive creations. These creations are literature, art, social symbols and ceremonials. They are like different dishes at one common feast. They add richness to our enjoyment and understanding of truth. They are making the world of man fertile of life and variedly beautiful.

But the nations do not create, they merely produce and destroy. Organisations for production are necessary. Even organisations for destruction may be so. But when, actuated by greed and hatred, they crowd away into a corner the living man who creates, then the harmony is lost, and the people's history runs at a break-neck speed towards some fatal catastrophe.

Humanity, where it is living, is guided by inner ideals; but where it is a dead organisation it becomes impervious to them. Its building process is only an external process, and in its response to the moral guidance it has to pass through obstacles that are gross and non-plastic

Man as a person has his individuality, which is the field where his spirit has its freedom to express itself and to grow. The professional man carries a rigid crust around him which has very little variation and hardly any elasticity. This professionalism is the region where men specialise their knowledge and organise their power, mercilessly elbowing each other in their struggle to come to the front. Professionalism is necessary, without doubt; but it must not be allowed to exceed its healthy limits, to assume complete mastery over the personal man, making him narrow and hard, exclusively intent upon pursuit of success at the cost of his faith in ideals.

In ancient India professions were kept within limits by social regulation. They were considered primarily as social necessities, and in the second place as the means of livelihood for individuals. Thus man, being free from the constant urging of unbounded competition, could have leisure to cultivate his nature in its completeness.

The Cult of the Nation is the professionalism of the people. This cult is becoming their greatest danger, because it is bringing them enormous success, making them impatient of the claims of higher ideals. The greater the amount of success, the stronger are the conflicts of interest and jealousy and hatred which are aroused in man's minds, thereby making it more and more necessary for other peoples, who are still living, to stiffen into nations. With the growth of nationalism, man has become the greatest menace to man. Therefore the continual presence of panic goads that very national ism into ever-increasing menace.

—— Rabindranath Tagore: "The Nation", *Creative Unity*

Macmillon & Co., Limited, London 1962. pp. 143-146

A consumer conscious society as it is today everywhere in the world needs the education of austerity in every walk of life. A synchronized pattern of social life christened in co-operation with the elements of simplicity, modesty and inherent contentment and ably supplemented and enriched with Truth, Beauty and Goodness acts as a practical guide to advancement of humanism. And so, when we speak of national development, it must essentially be brone in mind that education moulds the people of the nation and, for that end in view, the society by preparing them to be ready for greater sacrifice through intrinsic exercise of freedom. The inherent spirit of freedom as Tagore time and again makes us aware, is the only avenue of preparation for every human being to become really and significantly social. This spirit of freedom is, indeed, the spirit of social regeneration of humanity. Through this spirit everyone is enriched with the aura of social oneness irrespective or respective of caste, creed, religion etc., which are nothing but apparent constraints of effulgence of individuality. The crisis of modernity is the crisis of education which even now fights shy of making a significant contribution to social harmony and intrinsic exercise of freedom. As Tagore reminds us:

> What is of greatest value in case of human aspiration can never be unpursuable. And I do believe in this. If the freedom of our nation does not lie beside, it must lie above. We must not forget it even for a single movement. To expand all around by spreading branches, shoots is becoming our object of vision, and, for this, we have assumed it to be the only criterion for expand-

sion. But the movement upward is also the movement of life. Therein also the fruits of success are brought forth in fulness. The main point is: Whether this side or that, the attraction of vastness must be admitted. We will have to become great, and greater than what we are. We will have to give all ears to that corner, which strengthens us to easily sacrifice ourselves, which does not enclose our aspiration in the cage between the walls of the office and the job. When this movenent will be instilled in our national life, this force will become strong. Then, at every moment, we would begin to surmount our circumstances. Then no delicacies in our external conditions would slightly ashame us.

—— Rabindranath Tagore: "*Lakshya O Siksha*" ("Aims and Education"), *Siksha*, Visva-Bharti, 1973. p. 135.

[Translated be me.

What is therefore, essential for social regeneration and cohesion as an outcome of education is to ably and appropriately understand the true concept of freedom. Unfortunately, the contribution of a truly educated person to the society is fast losing ground due to the tremendous spurt of gadgets and amenities available at doorsteps within the twinkilng of an eye. And what is the picture of a synchronized, sane society? Here is a brilliant outline by Erich Fromm:

Modern man, if he dared to be articulate about his concept of heaven, would describe a vision which would look like the biggest departmental store in the world, showing new things and gadgets, and himself having plenty of money with which to buy them. He would wander around openmouthed in this heaven of gadgets and commodities, provided

> only that there were ever more and newer things to buy, and perhaps that his neighbours were just a little less privileged than he.
>
> ---**Erich Fromm** : *The Sane Society*, **Holt, Rinehart & Winston, Inc., New York 1955. p. 135**

To dwarf freedom is to dwarf the possibilities of sociọaesthentic poignance of humanism and cohesion. As a unique introspective visualizer of social synchronization of mankind, Tagore always affirms the fact that a single individual let loose in the sham exercise of freedom in affluence is meaningless and, therfore, a disgrace to the blessings of modern society. In education, what he actually wants to be worthily exercised and experimented upon is to do away with social diferences and invite all in the great and pompous feast of dissemination of knowledge and experience. Analysing the failures of our system of education in meeting the demands of the unenlightened and the neglected in the society, Tagore observes,

> The mostly admitted and at the same time mostly ignored fact about education is that education is living and not mechanical. The operational activities with regard to it may come afterwards, but the matter with reference to its living operations comes first of all. As the incubator machine is not easy, it is legion from the account of its strategies and expenditures. But as the laying of eggs by here is easy from natural principle of life, it does not allow exaggerations, and yet that is preferable.
>
> The continual desire to live and strive is the natural system of sustenance. The society where there is the force of life remains untiringly awake out of the urge for natural sticktoi-

> tiveness to the essential needs from the standpoint of self-protection; food and education, occupation and learning. People of the higher strata of society would be well nourished and satisfied with food and dress while those of the lower strata would remain halr fed or in starvation and the society would remain unconscious about that: it may be called as a paralysis of the half portion of the body. This disease of paralysis is the disease of barbarity.

——Rabindranath Tagore: "*Sikshar Swangikaran, Siksha,* Visva-Bharati. 1973. pp. 230-231

[Translated by me.

The education that nurtures such a disease of barbarity as Tagore elucidates above aggravates only social tension. Such differences in approach to dissemination of education tears apart all ideas of social cohesion. A sense of disbelief reigns supreme among all sections of people in the society who suffer from alienation both mentally and physically. A rift in emotional imbalance among people in the society shatters all their good intentions to have the blessings of a conjoint communicated living. Education remains a silent spectator in negotiating the darkness of ignorance and social superstitions looming large everywhere. Deeply pained at the appalling social inconsistencies, Tagore casts his aspersions on a hapless society that has pawned all its good intentions to accelerate and stabilize mass education and union of minds of all people of the society. As he observes

> That the irrigation in education would drench one or two inches only the upper class of the society and the corresponding lower strata of the society would cover the far ranging drought witn constant lifelessness with a thin veil : such a mind-annihilating utter foolishness has not

been idly accepted by a civilized society. Shame to that treacherous fortune of ours a hundred times that has compelled India to accept that.

There are certain planets and satellites which are in permanent dissociation from the one half part of darkness and light. Their one portion is towards the sun, the other, opposite to the sun. Likewise, the society in which there is the light of education in one part and the other greater part is bereft of education is cursed with self-separation. A difference of darkness invisible by the sun lies there between the educated and the uneducated. The difference in mind between them is more powerful than that of the two different types of men. The current of the one bank of the river is running towards the opposite direction of the current of the other bank of the same river. Their distance is more forcefully proved by the nearness of both of them.

—*Ibid* . pp. 131.232

[Translated by me

That to synchronize the mind of the country cannot be possible without a harmony of minds through education is one of the fundamental principles of Rabindranath's educational thoughts and experiments for promotion of social and national cohesion. The dissemination of education among the masses in the society is as he more often than not reminds us, not only essential but also mandatory. This is not a new endeavour but a process taken up for all-round accomplishments in right earnest from a backdrop of the Asian renaissance everywhere among the people in all sections of the so ciety. In a highly competitive and sensitive global society the harmony of human minds as well as an intelligent approach to exchange of social wealth and prosperity is all the more necessary for onward march of civilization and humanism. Here economic stringency is not a real constraint but a secondary matter of concern. With unity of education the social and national cohesion automatically follows. This is, as Tagore reminds us, the surest means to drive away drabness of mind and a certain sense of passivity among almost all persons in the society. Let the whole society be attuned with the spirit of oneness of social prosperity. Let the entire process of social synchronization be guided by education at all levels in a natural, comprehensive and fruitful manner. Then and then alone, education would be a useful means to bring about a lively social revolution.

It is interesting to note that as a social synchronizer Tagore does not dwarf his vision of socialism in narrowness of mere social and for that end in view, national outlook. Nor does he want to make education a mere tool for bringing about a bare change of social disparities. He strongly intends to bridge the gap between man and man by means of cultivating that inner spirit of education which makes man loyal to man. Socialism, then, adores true nationalism which in turn allows mankind to foster spiritual unity which serves as a guide to social harmony as well as to the continual endeavour for the ascent of man. Such nationalism based on dissemination of spiritual unity of mankind awaits education for acceleration of social harmony with a broad-based perspective of survival of mankind. As Tagore observes.

> During the evolution of the Nation the moral culture of brotherhood was limited by geographical boundaries, because at that time those boundaries were true. Now they have become imaginary lines of tradition divested of the qualities of real obstacles. So the time has come when man's moral nature must deal with

> this fact in all seriousness of perish. The first impulse of this change of circumstance has been the churning up of man's baser passions of greed and cruel hatred. If this persists indefinitely, and armaments go on exaggerating themselves to unimaginable absurdities, and machines and store-house envelop this fair earth with their dirt and smoke and ugliness, then it will end in a conflict of suicide. Therefore man will have to exert all his power of love and charity of vision to make another great moral adjustment which will comprehend the whole world of men and not merely the fractional groups of nationality. The call has come to every individual in the present age to prepare himself and his surroundings for this down of a new era, when man shall discover his soul in the spiritual unity of all human beings.

Rabindranath Tagore: *Nationalism* , Macmillan India Limited. New Delhi. 1950.

The education that caters to the socio-spiritual emancipation of man allows truth to liberate man from his little self and promotes him to foster his social and spiritual self of winning over all tempting components of materialism and utilitarianism. Let the *Parama Purusha* — the Person Supreme — be enkindled with the aesthetic aura of consciousness which transcends one from the domain of utilitarianism to that of true socialism that teaches the lesson of spiritual union of mind. Then alone man will understand the invaluable truth: *tena tyektena bhunjitha* "enjoy him through sacrifice". Then alone a man becomes ***man*** in the society through the aesthetic blessing of love and sympathy. Tagore makes a very characteristic exposure of this socio-aesthetic emancipation of man as follows:

> Our greed diverts our consciousness to

materials away from that supreme value of truth which is the quality of the universal being. The gulf thus created by the receding stream of the soul we try to replenish with a continuous stream of wealth, which may have the power to fill but not the power to unite and recreate. Therefore, the gap is dangerously concealed under the glittering quicksand of things, which by their own weight cause a sudden subsidence while we are in the depths of steep.

The real treagedy, however, does not lie in the risk of our material security but in the obscuration of Man himself in the human world. In the creative activities of his soul Man realizes his surroundings as his larger self, instinct with his own life and love. But in his ambition he deforms and defiles it with the callous handling of his voracity. His world of utility, assuming a gigantic proportion, reacts upon his inner nature and hypnotically suggests to him a scheme of the universe which is an abstract system. In such a world there can be no question of *mukti*, the freedom of truth, because it is a solitary fact, a cage with no sky beyond it. In all apprearance our world is a closed world of hard facts; it is like a seed with its tough cover. But within this enclsoure is working our silent cry of life for mukti, even when its possibility is darkly silent. When some huge overgrown temptation tramples into stillness this living aspiration then does civilization die like a seed that has lost its urging for germination. And this *mukti* is in the truth that dwells in the ideal man.

-Rabindranath Tagore: The Religion of Man, George Allien & Unwin Ltd. London 1951. pp. 72-73.

To seek the social man in his emancipation as an ideal man, the education that allows him to purify and prepare himself through self-sacrifice is the only way of social cohesion. That there is a close bond of social relationship between man and man is an instinctive urge of human relationship based on the true spirit of socialism, and Rabindranath directs our attention towards that particular aim and objective of education. Let education serve as a means of co-ordination between the country and the minds of men already alienated and even at cross-roads from manifold points of view. Let the learned and the ignorant in the society be endeared together by means of exercise of mutual bond of relationship which elminates all differences —social, cultural,etc. Let the truth of life emerge from that education which makes a harmony of human relationship a reality. As Rabindranath spells out the core of education for social cohesion in the light of the ancient Indian society,

> The forest that thrives itself by the living sustenance it recieves from the soil amply supplies the components of life all the time in spontaneity. It makes the latter continually alive. The fruits that it brings forth in the upper branches, the preparations for them in the soil below are an outcome of its own. Therefore,the soil of the forest turns out to be integrated with the forest; otherwise it would, being dissociated, have been a desert. Where the plant manure is not extended all over the soil, trees and plants grow there in scarcity and due to starvation become curved, twisted and thin. Once the contribution of the lofty trees in the social forest-land of our society was regularly showered upon the soil underneath. The western education that has now-a-days been introduced in our country has very meagrely contributed the soil. It is not making the land fertile by its own components. This very difference from coun-

> tries like Japan and so on is shameful and shocking. Our country is devoid of creating the role of her own education. Here the education of the country and her broad mind are dissociated from each other. In those days there was no antagonism of the nature of mind between the vastly learned scholars of the country and the illiterate villagers. A scholastic bent of mind in the latter has been built up. In that feast of learning and scholarship there were the partially fed all the time not by smelling but by enjoying the residues.

— Rabindranath Tagore : *"Sikshar Svangikaram"*, Visva-Bharati. 1973. pp. 233.

[Translated by me.

The education as Tagore always reminds, is like genuine sustenance of life that embraces society from every direction and involves all in the feast of advancement of humanism. It eliminates narrowness of mind, ignorance and apathy which, as he reminds with significant caution, are 'the worst forms of bondage for men'. As education acts like a living, pulsating sustenance to social advancement, its primary objective is to allow everyone in society to embrace it as one's very Hence the truth for social cohesion derived from living education—liberating the self for the Supreme Being in every person.

Education for social emancipation and social synchronization awaits the freedom of the individual, who is already hapless victim to veneration of the dead corpse of stifled socialism that is even nor rampant in a consumer-crushed careless society. Really, each one of us is Tagore's Amal in the *Post Office* caged and crippled in a suffocating society where we are simply hollow men having no reverence for the prized divinity in man. Moreover, for social cohesion in India culture of the soul in the ancient Indian pattern of social culture and tradition. The liberation of the human spirit thus made would enable everyone in society to be initiated with the ardent spirit of sympathy and service, kindness and co-operation, tolerance and devotion. The education that aims at such a social harmony would enable every person to discover and appreciate the inner divinity in man. Not mere informatics but a genuine inspiration and devotion to the well-being of oneself by means of entrusting with the well-being of others is the fundamental objective of education which for the sake of being meaningful must synchronize the intellectual and the physical aspects of man. When Tagore speaks of such a unity of the mind and the spirit, social coherence to be brought about through education to give importance to the educational thoughts and experiments of the ancient India whose primary concern is the culture of the soul by the pupils leading a simple and austere *ashram* life. Indeed, when Tagore introduces the ashramic pattern of education in his own school at Santiniketan, his primary objective is to initiate education for social regeneration by means of bringing about a radical change in education for the culture of the soul in the ancient Indian pattern of education for social consciousness and spiritual excellence.

---

* S. Radhakrishan makes an indepth analysis of Tagore's approach to man and society as follows :

> The vast social mechanism created by man is now crushing the soul. Independent thinking and individuality are suppressed. If like the child Amal in the *Post Office* we cripple our minds and narrow our freedom by confining it to our closed prisons and taking the directions of our traditional doctors, the Sastras, we shall not recover from our illusions. As the child longs to be out, mind craves for freedom.

But we have to break open the gates and pull down the walls of our closed house, for the air and light of God to pour and enlighten us.

Rabindranath does not view the social problems of the time from the narrow economic or utilitarian point of view. He brings his spiritual vision to bear on the social problems, and lifts them up to a higher idealist plane. His attitude to them is determined not by the accident of birth, habit, or training, but by the spiritual vision, the one central principle to which he devoted his whole life. The present social unrest would be at an end if people adopted the right attitude to life, and developed reverence for the devine.

—S. Radhakrishnan: *The Philosophy of Rabindranath Tagore,* Good Companions Publishers, Borada, India. 1961. p. 115.

The ideal which India possessed in the past should come back in its essence, though not in its entirety. "The highest education is that which does not merely give us information but makes our life in harmony with all existence" (*The spirit of Japan,* p. 116)." The object of education is to give man the unity of truth. Formerly when life was simple, all the different elements of man were in complete harmony. But when there came the separation of the intellect from the spiritual and the physical, the school education put entire emphasis on intellect and the physical side of man. We devote our sole attention in giving children information, not knowing that by this emphasis we are accentuating a break between the intellectual, physical, and the spiritual life.

(*Ibid*. p. 126). But how is the spiritual life to be cultivated? Not by means of any set of lessons about God and His existence but by allowing the souls to express themselves free and spontaneously. Rabindranath trusts the instinct of the pupil and the atmosphere of the *ashram* for the kindling of the spiritual aspiration and the development of the spiritual life. "With the breath we draw we must always feel the truth, that we are living in God." (*Ibid*). In ancient India it was possible, because in the *ashram* which is home, school, temple and forest rolled into one, the teachers were men who every moment felt the presence of God and lived their life to Him. So their pupils felt God as they felt the green of the earth or the blue of the sky. Education, which aims at the emancipation of the soul and the liberation of the human spirit from its trammels, would open the eyes of Indians to the enormous waste of life, health, and spirit, which daily takes place in the country; would reveal to them the complete circumscription of opportunity, and would give them the courage of heart and strength of mind to fight injustice in every form. In his school at Bolpur, which is not only a school of culture but an abode of piety and a school of art, Rabindranath combines modern methods of education with the ancient Indian ideal of soul-culture. To him the ideal school "Must be an ashram where men have gathered together for the highest end of life, in the peace of nature; where life is not merely mediative but fully awake in its activities, where boys' minds are not perpetually drilled into believing that the ideal of the self-idolatry of the nation is the truest ideal for them to accept; where they are bidden to realise man's world as God's kingdom to whose citizenship they have to aspire; where the sunrise and sunset and the silent glory of the stars are not daily ignored; where nature's festivities of flowers and fruit have their joyous recognition from man; and where the young and the old, the teacher and the student, sit at the same table to partake of their daily food and the food of their eternal life" (*Ibid.* p. 148).

S. Radhakrishnan: *The Philosophy of RabindranathTagore,* Good Companions Publishers, Baroda, India.1961. pp. 127-128.

Education to be truly effective for social synchronization must cultivate the education of the soul which indeed is the soul of education. Tagore draws our attention towards that education which teaches as the lesson of mutual understanding and tolerance, respect and poignance. The relation between the teacher and the taught should be essentially based on this revelation of truth that there must be a harmony between whatever we learn and wherever we do as a practical exposure of learning. Tagore is deeply grieved at the painful failure of the role of education in bringing about awareness to the social instinct of ardent mutual relationship berween the teacher and the taught and the impact of education upon the society. As a matter of fact, he points out attention towards the formidable position arising out of social disparities where education remains inactive and silent, inoperative and passive. A mechanical pursuit of education only allows sham display of intellect unrelated to social development. Consequently, the society nurtures only dissociation of sensibilities and utter disparities in approach to life. Tagore delineates this point very distinctly:

Where the society has not made the avenues of its own healthy synchronization with the current of life, and so, where the arrangements of the olden times are acting like constraints and arresting its course, the educational institution most natural and broadened at that place is not only not in favour of us but also more formidable than that: it exists and yet it is extinct, it does not allow truth to have its avenue and accumulates falsehood. This society does not at all want to admit movement, and as such, makes existence polluted.

Such is the enclosed condition of the social school and next to it is the royal school. That, too, is an enormous stereotyped affair. Its only endeavour is to consolidate all the principles of the country in the same mould. Therefore, this big machinery of learning is becoming a machine for clerkship. Man is heaping here the sacks of degrees of picking up the pebbles of notes, but that is not the food for life. Its glory lies in the glory of burdening, and not in the glory of life.

Rabindranath Tagore: "*Sikshavidhi*," *Siksha*, Visva-Bharati, 1973. p. 127

[Translated by me.

The education that suffers from such a cronic disease of maladjustment between the ideal and the real, the principle and the practice as we even now come across in so-called educational institutions cannot but embrace a schizophrenic society where man becomes a passive observer to falsehood and injustice, hypocrisy and greed. Education, then, is batered in terms of material gains — a mechanical tool to prize pupils with degrees, diplomas and certificates only to make a robotized society of lifelessness and crudity. The inner truth in man in the society pines away in the melee of utilitarian affluence. Tagore refers to this dangerous symp tom which has drifted education away from its main purpose: to make the learner aware of the finer sensibilities within him, to allow him to open out his mind in full freedom of atmosphere, and to enable him to undertake the spirit of adventure in the society to which he belongs. As he categorically observes,

> Our system of education refuses to admit that children are children. Children are punished because they fail to behave like grown-up people and have the impertinence to be noisily childish. Their educators do not know, or they refuse to acknowledge that this childishness is Nature s own provision and that the child through its restless mind and movements should always come into touch with new facts and stumble upon new information. Thus the child becomes the battle-ground for a fight between the school master and Mother Nature herself.The school master is of opinion that the best means of educating a child is by concentration on mind, but Mother Nature knows that the best way is dispersion of mind. When we were children, we came to gather facts by such scattering of mental energy, through unexpected surprises. The surprise gave us that shock which was needed to make us intensely conscious of the facts of life, of the world. Facts must come fresh to children to startle their minds into full activity.
>
> It is the utter want of purpose in child-life which is important. In adult age, having made our life a bundle of a few definite purposes, we exclude all facts outside their boundaries. Our purpose wants to occupy all the mind's attention for itself, obstructing the full view of most of the things around us; it cuts a narrow

bed for our deliberate mind which seeks its end through a restricted passage. The child, because it has no conscious object of life beyond living, can see all things around it, can hear every sound with a perfect freedom of attention, not having to exercise choice in the collection of information. It gives full reign to its restlessness which leads its mind into knocking against knowledge.

I have a deep-rooted conviction that only through freedom can man attain his fulness of growth, and when we restrict that freedom it means that we have some purpose of our own which we impose on our children, and we have not in mind Nature's own purpose of giving the child its fulness of growth.

If we have some purpose expressed through our educational institutions — that children should be producing patriots, practical men, soldiers, bankers, then it may be necessary that we have to put them through the mechanical drill of obedience and discipline! But that is not the fulness of life not the fulness of humanity. He who knows that Nature's own purpose is to make the boy a full man when he grows — full in all directions, mentally and mainly spiritually — he who realises this, brings up the child in the atmosphere of freedom.

Rabindranath Tagore: "The School Master" *The Modern Review*, Calcutta, October, 1924. pp. 369-372.

The lesson of education for social cohesion as Tagore intensely feels and experiences should always be imparted in exercise of freedom in the midst of Nature. It must follow and never precede, the spotaneous growth and development of the child who makes self-analysis and self-study in its reatio to the social atmosphere to which it is attached. The surrounding world beckons a child to have its first experience rich in awe and wonder, poignance and promise. Bereft of such education, the experiences to be derived through natural events and consequences remain blurred and barricaded in the four walls of a school which is nothing but a *'dasta-panchtar Andaman"* a ten-to-five prison house as Tagore rightly comments. Indeed, he expresses his great sense of relief when he says about himself:

> I had been blessed with that sense of wonder which gives a child his right of entry into the treasure-house of mystery which is the heart of existence. I neglected my studies because they rudely summoned me away from the world around me, which was my friend and my companion, and when I was thirteen I freed myself from the clutch of an educational system that tried to keep me imprisoned within the stonewalls of lessons.
>
> I had a vague notion as to who or what it was that touched my heart's chords, like the infant which does not know its mother's name, or who or what she is. The feeling which I always had was a deep satisfaction of personality that flowed into my nature through living channels of communication from all sides.
>
> It was a great thing for me that my consciousness was never dull about the facts of the surrounding world. That the cloud was the cloud, that flower was a flower, was enough, because they directly spoke to me, because I could not be indifferent to them. I still remem

> ber the very moment, one afternoon when coming back from school I alighted from the carriage and suddenly saw in the sky, behind the upper terrace of our house, an exhuberance of deep, rain-clouds lavishing rich, cool shadows on the atmosphere. The marvel of it, the very generosity of its presence, gave me a joy which was freedom, the freedom we feel in the love of our dear friend.

Rabindranath Tagore: *The Religion of An Artist*, Visva-Bharti Bookshop, Calcutta. Reprinted from *Contemporary Indian Philosophy*, George Allen & Unwin Ltd. 1953. pp. 10-11.

Admittedly, education for manifestation of freedom of mind in the right perspective of social awareness makes it meaningful and conducive to individual creative and social excellence. The schools for academic excellence necessitate an approach to real social happenings in and around the pupils for whom a diverse flow of experience and avenue of innovations must always cater to individual creativity and social poignance.

The socio-creative mind of man seeking emancipation from the so-called modernity that makes us victims dullness and passivity awaits a revolution within to counteract against all forces standing in the way of the freedom of the inner spirit of man and society. When Tagore speaks of the role of education for promotion of social harmony he stabilizes his viewpoints from an introspective approach to man as creative artist. The vision of true modernism as he depicts is the vision of man reborn in the ashes of consumerism and the poignance of freedom of the modern mind nursed in an ideal conjoint and communicated social life. If education fails to be a sincere partner to such synchronization between man and society, it becomes a dead lump of bookish learning that always betrays the artist in each man of revolutionalized and reenkindled modern society. As Tagore characteristical observe,

The races of man have poetry in their heart and it is necessary for them to give, as far as possible, a perfect expression to their sentiments. For this they must have a medium, moving and pliant, which can freshly become their very own, age after age. All great languages have undergone and are still undergoing changes. Those languages which resist the spirit of change are doomed and will never produce great harvests of thought and literature. When forms become fixed, the spirit either weakly accepts its imprisonment within them or rebels. All revolutions consist of the fight of the within against invasion by the without.

There was a great chapter in the history of life on this earth when some irresistible inner force in man found its way out into the scheme of things, and sent forth its triumphant mutinous voice, with the cry that it was not going to be overwhelmed from outside by huge brute beast of a body. How helpless it appeared at the moment, but has it not nearly won? In our social life also, revolution breaks out when some power concentrates itself in outside arrangements and threatens to enslave for its own purpose the power which we have within us.

When an organization which is a machine becomes a central force, political, commercial, educational or religious, it obstructs the free flow of inner life of the people and waylays and exploits it for the augmentation of its own power. Today, such concentration of power is fast multiplying on the outside and the cry of the oppressed spirit of man is in the air which struggles to free itself from the grip of screws and bolts, of unmeaning obsessions.

> Revolution must come and men must risk revilement and misunderstanding, especially from those who want to be comfortable, who put their faith in materialism, and belong truly to the dead past and not modern times, the past that had its age in distant antiquity when physical flesh and size predominated, and not the mind of man.
>
> Purely physical dominance is mechanical and modern machines are merely exaggerating our bodies, lengthening and multiplying our limbs. The modern mind, in its innate childishness, delight in this enormous bodily bulk, representing an ordinate material power, saying: "Let me have the big toy and no sentiment which can disturb it". It does not realize that in this we are returning to that antidiluvian age which revelled in its production of gigantic physical frames, leaving no room for the freedom of the inner spirit.

—Rabindranath Tagore: *The Religion Of An Artist*, Visva-Bharati Bookshop, Calcutta. 1953. pp. 4-5. Reprinted from *Contemporary Indian Philosophy*, George Allen & Unwin Ltd.

True socialism as Tagore thinks and translates into action in his own experimentations on education for rural reconstruction and social awareness at Shelaidah (now in Bangladesh) and Sriniketan, is essentially based on the dignity of the inner spirit of man. Let man think, feel and activate himself with the changing social needs and priorities but never at the cost of loss of inner freedom or identity. Let him feel the pulse of the society not by opening alien thoughts and experimentations but by exploring newer dimensions of education for social revolution by taking recourse to rich indigenous socio-cultural heritage and tradition. When Tagore speaks of living education he ardently incorporates that type of education which has its roots in the very core of the indigenous society and which caters to the innovations and experimentations on the basis of original indigenous needs and priorities to usher forth a new enlivening spirit of social cohesion. It is interesting to note that what Tagore hails as nurturing the social wishes and aspiration through cultivation of indigenous social and intellectual spirit of enquiry rather than being 'trampled down under the dead pressure of a mechanical method and the callous contemputous discouragement' is now being warmly appreciated by our country men who strongly feel the importance of austerity and simplicity as favourable grounds for efflorescence of originality. The living social outlook of scientists like Jagadischandra Bose and Acharya Prafullachandra Ray as he directs our attention to, might make us aware of the appropriate role of education for the cause of social integration and social welfare. Analysing the causes of failure of the National Council of Education of the preindependence India, he says:

> No one has been able to give us a complete definition of life, because, at every moment, it transcends its parts and is mysteriously more than what we get from its analysis. What it gives out is far greater in quality and value, than the materials it consumes. It is not a mere sum total of the carbon, nitrogen and other ingradients which it takes in with its food. Our mind, also in the fulness of its life, is infinitely greater than the information it appropriates, the training it acquires. That education is true, which acknowledges the mind to be a living thing, and therefore stimulates it to give out more in quality and quantity than is imparted to it from outside. And we are to judge our education by this standard.

Therefore the question is, whether, in our intellectual career in the modern time, we have given more than we have received, and created something which is our own. For when any race of men becomes a mere burden in the world, rendering no satisfactory account of the cost it imposes upon the society, this, for it, is worse than death. For this is the intolerably mean situation of remaining under the charge of perpetual misappropriatior

As for us, far from having given our University more than we received, we have not even rendered back full measure. We have been repeating great words, learning great truths looking on great examples, but in turn we have simply become clerks, deputy magistrates, pleaders or physicians.

Not that it is a small thing to be, for instance, a physician. But though our physicians are now practising in every town and village and hamlet of the country and though many of them are of good repute and making money, all this extensive experience of theirs has not resulted in any new theory, or great fact, being added to the science of medicine. Like good school-boys, they have only applied with over-cautious precision just what they have learnt. And who shall make good the vital thing that is lost when students never become masters?

Yet I cannot admit that this is due to any inherent defect in our natural powers. There was a long period in the past, during which the science of healing with us was a living growth,

> spreading its different off-school and branches all over our country. That teaches us at least this much that in those days our mind was in living connection with its acquirements; that, then, we did not merely learn by rote, but made our own observations and experiments; that we tried to discover principles and build hypotheses and apply them to life.
>
> Where has this initiative and courage of ours have departed? Why do we tread so carefully, so fearfully, under the load of our learning? Is it because we were born to be serfs, permanently bending under the burden of another's intellectual acquisitions? Never!
>
> For even in spite of the scarceness of opportunities and narrowness of prospects, in spite of our present defective education, which has been starved of all life elements, a few great men of science like Jagadischandra and Prafullachandra, and a great scholar like Brajendranath, have made their appearance in our country, proving that the power of true originality is not lacking among our people, only it is trampled down under the dead pressure of a mechanical method and the callousness of comtemptuous discouragement.

—— Rabindranath Tagore: *The Centre of Indian Culture,* Visva-Bharti Bookshop, Calcutta. 1951. pp. 9-11.

What makes education truly social in approach? What are its social responsibilities? How can it inculcate social awareness to bring about a radical change in the society by baptising a man to 'men'? How can the educational programmes be geared to involve a pupil to be socially conscious of his relationship with others. All these and numerous other social problems that await the real involvement of education never avert the introspective vision of Tagore as practical social thinker and experimenter. When he lays emphsis on rural development the ideas that primarily play a significant role are always with close reference to rural art, culture, industry, health, hygiene, recreation and so on which suffer a lot from indignities and apathy. His first concern is, therefore, mass reorientation and revitalization by means of dissemination of education in all these directions so that the rural society might revive its lost social prestige and position in the mainstream of the country and the world at large. His experimentations on education to meet the ends in view at Sriniketan and at her neighbouring villages bear significant evidence of his uncompromising zeal and untiring endeavour even at the cost of incomparable individual creative sensibilities. He brings about a certain change in qualitative education for rural people when he introduces new ideas self-help, self-activity, creativity and self-development in educational plans and programmes of activities like organisation of physical education through *Brati-Balak* and *Brati-Balika* organisations, learning of self-defence through games like Judo, acrobatics, stick-play, knife-plays, and numerous other indigenous games and sports. Side by side with these, he revitalizes the rural masses by means of reintroducing the socio-cultural and socio-spiritual elements of human development by means of *Kirtan*, *Baul*, Mela and other social congregations where people irrespective of cast, creed, religion, etc. exchange their views and appreciation in a cordial social atmosphere. As for advancement of theoretical leaning in the direction of social cohesion, he introduces *Chalantika* (Rural Circulating Library), *Lokasiksha Samsad* (Society for Mass Education), Night Schools, Rural Adult-education centres enriched with easy-to-read and graded books on diverse subjects written by eminent scholars and experts in different disciplines. Tagore himself contributes abundantly towards broadening the rural minds and widening their outlook by writing books and pamphlets like *Visva-Parichay*, *Palli Prakritti* etc. which show how devoted and sincere he is in undertaking a Herculean task of lauching an adventure into the inner as well as the outer world of rural people to accelerate and enrich their social thinking and social harmony*. Not only this but he also wants to infuse a new spirit of social oneness through education that has amply provided a wave of enthusiasm among all sections of people in society to emerge as men enjoying and enriching a conjoint, communicated global life and global society. The inner social spirit of the mind of man must, as he strongly feels and advocates be allowed a wider sky of freedom for efflorescence for exercise of creative vision and invaluable individuality so that there is a genuine possibility and perfection of the onward march for all-round social harmony and social excellence. In this sense, Tagore is absolutely right when he strongly asserts that a single man, being merely and literally single, is entirely meaningless. The spirit of altruism in every person, indeed, lies dormant and it is the fundamental objective of education to create a social atmosphere of cohesion and mutual exchange of ideas and ideals to enable him to come out of his little self and amply contribute to the social self.

When Tagore introduces the co-operative societies and the co-operative banks for promotion of rural economy, the inherent purpose is to bring about the spirit of social harmony and go ahead with newer visions of an egalitarian society where everyone wholeheartedly devotes himself to the excellence and furtherance of man as 'men'. Tracing the history of India, he refers to the need for marriage of the constructive skill of the West with the creative and social spirit of the East. And for real emergence of the coherent social man, education must make a pivotal role to disseminate the spirit of hospitality for which India can always claim the supreme role. Tagore hints at this point as follows :

> When individual communities who come
> to dwell in the same neighbourhood, differ

* See Page 179

> from each other in race and culture the first attempts at unity become too obviously mechanical in their classified compartments. Some system of adjustment is needed in kinds of society, but in order that a system should be successful it must completely submit itself to the principle of life and become the organ for the vital functions.
>
> The history of India has been the history of the struggle between the constructive spirit of the machine, which seeks the cadence or order and conformity in social organization and the creative spirit in man, which seeks freedom and love for its self-expression. We have to watch and see if the latter is still living in India; and also whether the former offers its service and hospitality of life, through which its system can be vitalized.

--- Rabindranath Tagore : *A Vision of India's History,* Visva-Bharati Bookshop. Calcutta. 1951 p. 1.

A greater extension of the social oneness of man as Tagore visualizes, is the most vital role of education towards which all our attention and endeavour should, with all sincerity of purpose, be directed. This is particularly relevant in case of education in India that always aims at unfolding and disseminating truth throughout the global society for mutual understanding and co-operation, patience and promotion of humanism. Education for social harmony, therefore, awaits enrichment and expansion of individuality. As Tagore remarks,

> The age in which we now live, we cannot

> see clearly its true features, as from without. Yet we feel that the India of today has roused herself once more to search out her truth, her harmony, her oneness, not only among her own constituent elements, but with great world. The current of her life, which had been the dammed up in stagnation, has found some breach in the wall and can feel the pulse of the tidal wave of humanity outside. We shall learn thatt we can reach the great world of man not through the effacement but through the expansion of our individuality. We shall now for certain that just as it is futile mendicancy to covet the wealth of others in place of our own, so also to keep ourselves segregated and starved by refusing the gift which is the common heritage of man because it is brought by a foreign messenger, only makes for utter destitution.
>
> —*ibid*. p. 36

At the same time, Tagore, for the first time as a social visionary, directs our attention towards pettiness of mind and outlook in our endeavour to dissociate ourselves from the mainstream of society by means of following and translating into reality education for bare livelihood and maintaining a carefree, casual and disinterested approach to life as it is even now followed in a consumer-oriented utilitarian and selfish society. Education there has a very serious role to play, otherwise the social aims and objectives of education cannot but be dwarfed and scissored for a selfish approach to life and tainted in avarice and narrowness of vision. The education we receive through books remain far away from the education that we could have attained by means of having rich and diverse experience in social interactions, and the society might usher forth a new wave of enthusiasm to social synchronization. This is, indeed, a very arduous task of education, for its necessitates learning the different symptoms of social disharmony, experiencing the social life of the people in the different corners of the country and the world slowly but accurately, directly or indirectly thereby making the rule of education justified to the cause of desirable and functional socialization and humanism. It is interesting to note in this connection that, nearly eighty years ago, Tagore referred to these aims and of objectives of education in terms of social evolution and global human welfare :

> We have nothing more to want. The society is not beckoning us towards a greater cause, a greater sacrifice. Besides observing some artificial and meaningless rules related to rising and sitting, taking food and touching, it does not want any account from us in any other matter.

* * * *

> As we do not visualize the sphere of life in a broader canvas, we never feel the need for enlarging life and sacrifice for its cause in a greater span. Whatever thought we endeavour for this purpose is bookish, whateve work we intend to do is an imitation of others.

* * * *

> We are unfortunate in the sense that as others express doubt about us and as we fail to have any measure to prove that doubt false, there is a sense of doubt which becomes deep-

rooted in our minds as well. In this way the man who loses faith in himself cannot even endeavour at crossing any river; he roams about within a limited sphere near the bank and remains satisfied with this

* * * *

You are greater than a clerk, a munsef; whatever you are learning is not, like the shooting firework in the sky, meant for flying up to the profession of a school master somehow or other and ending like ashes, in being worn out in enjoying pensions' -- to stick to this dictum in education is the most essential one in our country and this should be borne in mind by every one of us all the time. The ignorance arising out of our failure to society fails to make us understand this fact, nor is this education available in our schools as well.

—Rabindranath Tagore: "*Lakshya O Siksha*" *Siksha,* Vishva Bharati. 1973. pp. 131-132.

[Translated by me.

How far do we follow Rabindranath's suggestions for promotion of national cohesion through living eduction?

---

*Here is an illiminating analysis of Rabindranath as a practical exponent of dissemination of education for promotion of social harmony and social regeneration:

> The education programme of Santiniketan and Sriniketan amply manifested the essential ideas characterizing Tagore's approach to educational sociology. The manifold educational activities of Sriniketan, through a separate education department as well as through allied activities of departments, and the care and thoroughness and with which they had been planned and executed, prove Tagore's firm faith in education as the primary factor in the regeneration of the masses.

All this relates to the programme of benefiting the society through education. But the parallel problem of giving fulness to education through living contact with the society was also equally attended to, as borne out by the ideals of education that inspired the activities of the institutions at Santiniketan and Sriniketan. In accordance with Tagore's view that an educational institution should be rooted to the native soiil, the pattern of life and education as conceived at the Santiniketan school was essentially in the line with Indian traditions, which at once distinguished it from a typical Anglo-Vernacular school of that time, based on the imitation of western models. Its curriculum and methods of teaching reflected the life and traditions of the Indian people in general to whom the school belonged, as also the objects of interests in the life of the local community and the flora and fauna of the area in particular where the school was situated. The teachers and students of Santiniketan were led to think of their institution as a part of the habitation around it and to take active interest in its needs and problems. It was also inculcated in them that they should induce the neighbouring population to regard the institution as their own and to participate in various activities of the institution. This approach was much more accentuated with the establishment of Sriniketan which became a living centre for social contact through multiple means. The direct contact with the life and problems of the villagers and the common people, which was encouraged among the members of the institutions, not only served to impart freshness, accuracy, and reality to their knowledge, but it also enriched their personality through broadening their experience and enlarging their sympathy. Life at Santiniketan and Sriniketan having been moulded after the pattern of a large family, various social qualities and virtues came to be intensely cultivated there. The students to those institutions soon acquired considerable reputation for their qualitiies of sociability, helpfulness, hospitality, and agreeable manners. They also acquired socially useful skills like fire-fighting, flood-fighting, and controlling crowds during fairs and festivals. The socio-economic usefulness of particular courses of training also received considerable emphasis at Sriniketan, and while Tagore's ideal of complete education was never entirely forgotten educational efforts were directed towards the ideal of social fitness and economic efficiency with a view to the students' attaining successful and fruitful membership of a dynamic community. Finally, the general atmosphere and day-to-day life in all the institutions were sweetened by the breath of democracy, so that distinctions of caste and social position were kept at a distance. There was little suggestion of the employer and the employees in the relationship between the authorities and workers of institutions, and there was little distinction between the high and the low in official hierarchy among the workers themselves. Teachers and students also mixed freely and cordially with one another, ignoring the traditional relationship of dignified distance that the former maintained with the latter at other places. Even the servants and the menials were led to feel at home with all the rest, and on the *Punyaha* Day, the 10th of March, every year, teachers and students took over the entire job of the menials and not only gave them an off-day but actually served them by feeding and entertaining them. Though, one may assume, there must have been occasional lapeses from this tradition in that large community comprising a diversity of people, the ideal, nonetheless, was there, living and active, imparting to the institution as a whole the character of a truly democratic society bound together by the spirit of equality, goodwill, and respect for one another.

—H. B. Mukherjee:*Education for Fulness*, Asia Publishing House, Bombay. 1962. pp. 313-314.

5

EDUCATION FOR SOCIO-MYSTIC FULFILMENT

TAGOREAN POIGNANCE

Education is always a quest within. It is a quest unending, challenging, introspective, and appreciative to the greatness of humanity. It allows mankind to live in mutually shared platform of living vision of truth: the glory of man who by exercise of erudition and experience accelerates thc beyonding of man

Enriched with the crystallized experience of the socio-mystic advancement of man, Tagore evaluated education in terms of restoration of the inner growth of mankind through education that caters to the quest for socio-spiritual and socio-mystic advancement. The horrors of the last two world wars have deeply pained him. The escalation of the two .

hemispheres the East and the West, from different dismensions — social, moral, spiritual, economic and so on — has only brought about a sense of desolation and hollowness of mind where education has remained, as it is more or less even now, a dump witness. An utter sense of hopelessness and greed has already overpowered the finer sentiments and softer visions of mankind, where education is yet to play its vital role. A robotized and schizophrenic society eats up the inner essence of the eternal mystery of man while education is doped in utilitarianism and consumerism.

A socio-mystic visionary *par excellence,* Tagore portrays the agonising picture of this global erosion of the inner depth of vision of mankind and paves a positive line of approach to this crucial problem by spelling out the true function of university:

> It is not the fear of danger or loss to one people or another, however, which is most important. The demoralising influence of the constant estrangement between the two hemispheres, which affects the baser passions of man, — pride, greed and hypocrisy on the one hand; fear, suspiciousness and flattery on the other, — has been developing, and threatens us with a world-wide spiritual disaster.
>
> The time has come when we must use all our wisdom to understand the situation, and to control it, with a stronger trust in moral guidence than in any array of physical forces.
>
> In the beginning of man's history his first social object was to form a community, to grow into a people. At that early period, individuals were gathered together within geographical enclosures. But in the present age, with its facility of communication, geograph-

ical barriers have almost lost their reality, and the great federation of men, which is waiting either to find its true scope or to break asunder in a final catastrophe, is not a meeting of individuals, but of various human races. Now the problem before us is of one single country, which is the earth, where the races as individuals must find both their freedom of self-expression and their bond of federation. Mankind must realise a unity, wider in range, deeper in sentiment, stronger in power than ever before. Now that the problem is large, we have to solve it on a bigger scale, to realise the God in man by a larger faith and to build the temple of our faith on a sure and world-wide basis.

The first step towards realisation is to create opportunities for revealing the different peoples to one another. This can never be done in those fields where the exploiting utilitarian spirit is supreme. We must find some meeting ground, where there can be no question of conflicting interests. One of such places is the University, where we can work together in a common pursuit of truth, share together our common heritage, and realise that artists in all parts of the world have created forms of beauty, scientists discovered secrets of the universe, philosophers solved the problems of existence, saints made the truth of the spiritual world organic in their own lives, not merely for some particular race to which they belonged but for all mankind. We must know that the great mind of man is one, working through the many differences which are needed to ensure the full result of its fundamental unity. When we understand this truth in a disinterested spirit, it teaches us to respect all the differences in man that are real,

> yet remain conscious of our oneness; and to know that perfection of unity is not in uniformity, but in harmony.

— Rabindranath Tagore: "An Eastern University," *Creative Unity*, Macmillan & Co.Ltd., London 1922. pp. 170-172.

The purpose of education to allow the learner to enter deep into the inner world of mankind and foster the spirit of excellence of intrinsic harmony is long overdue. Mankind must search for the eternal light within, the insatiable spirit of adventure within, the quest for the beauty of each 'I' and 'We' within, the perfection of goodness within and, to do so, education must serve as an effective and stimulating tool. The society in which we live today lacks the vigour that it should derive out of the stimulating components of education which might allow everyone to regain the lost depth of inner vision and might be rejuvenated with a new spirit of unending quest for evaluating indigenous social art, culture and heritage, education, aesthetics, and ethical values. Tagore, for example, draws our attention towards indigenous folk culture, the scriptures, the epics and the *Puranas*, old religious literature and so on prove the fact that education must embrace all these to regain the inherent glory of harmony—the inner spirit that allows the beyonding of man. Added to these, is the typical avenue of simplicity of life-process as depicted in diverse folk-education towards which Tagore draws our attention

> Where society is comparatively simple and obstructions are not too numerous, we can clearly see how the life process guides education in its vital purpose. The system of folk-education, which is indigenous to India, but is dying out, was one with the people's life. It flowed naturally through the social channels and made its way everywhere. It is a system of widespread irrigation of culture. Its teachers,

especially trained men, are in constant requisition, and find crowded meetings in our villages, where they repeat the best thoughts and express the ideals of the land in the most effective form. The mode of instruction include the reaction of epics, expounding of the scriptures, reading from the Puranas, which are the classical records of old history, performance of plays founded upon the early myths and legends, dramatic narration of the lives of ancient heroes, and the singing in chorus of songs from the old religious literature. Evidently, according to this system, the best function of education is to enable us to realise that to live as a man is great, requiring profound philosophy for its idea, peotry for its expression, and heroism in its conduct. Owing to this vital method of culture the common people of India, though technically illiterate, have been made conscious of the sanctity of social relationships, entailing constant sacrifice and self-control, urged and supported by ideals collectively expressed in one word, *Dharma.*

Such a system of education may sound too simple for the complexities of modern life. But the fundamental principle of social life in its different stages of development remains the same; and in no circumstance can the truth be ignored that all human complexities must harmonise in organic unity with life, failing which there will be endless conflict. Most things in the civilised world occupy more than their legitimate space. Much of their burden is needless. By bearing this burden civilised man may be showing great strength, but he displays little skill. To the gods,viewing this from on high, it must seem like the flounderings of a giant who

> has got out of his depth and knows not how to swim.
>
> *Ibid.* pp. 182-183.

The system of education that was in vogue in ancient India was a system of maintaining and enriching the living truth of man and society — a truth that expanded the socio-mystic horizon of the human mind. It is a system of education that awaits re-thinking and regeneration of the society in the context of harmonization of human complexities with the organic unity of life. Education must unfold Truth. It must not be a mere tool for informatics but inspire every learner to be a real partner to the society as well as an ardent follower of Truth to appreciate its wonder and infinity. Education, then, becomes a genuine vehicle of socio-mystic fulfilment. It teaches how to live, as true education should always have this primary objective for this end in view. What is of greater significance is the role of the teacher. What should a teacher do for education of the learner for socio-mystic advancement ? Should he merely impart knowledge and deal with 'dead specimens of once living things' ? Here is Tagore's observation:

> A most important truth, which we are apt to forget, is that a teacher can never truly teach unless he is still learning himself. A lamp can never light another lamp unless it continues to burn its own flame. The teacher who has come to the end of his subject, who has no living traffic with knowledge, but merely repeats his lessons to his students, can only load their minds; he cannot quicken them. Truth not only must inform but inspire. If the inspiration dies out, and the information only accumulates then truth loses its infinity. The greater part of our learning in schools has been washed because, for most of our teacher, their subjects are like,

> dead specimens of once living things, with which they have a learned acquaintance, but no communication of life and love.

— Rabindranath Tagore: "An Eastern University", *Creative Unity*, Macmillan Co. Ltd. London 1962, pp. 186 187.

Education for restoration and cultivation of Truth in the society is the *sine qua non* of an enlightened vision of global mankind. True education always caters to the all round devolpment of the inner mind that highlights the Truth of the individual with the Truth of the Universal. It synchronizes the necessities of inner growth and development with the beyonding of man. Therein lies the excellence of education in guiding an individual to see within and see into the light of beyonding of consciounsness in the society. Is education becomes such a vehicle of qualitative and quantitative advancement of the individual from all dimensions of human development, the promise of efflorescence of the All Serene in an altruistic society becomes a living reality. Then we will have the genuine concept of education as a living spirit of humanism and more than toying with that bare information which is eating up the vitalities of inner life. Let education unfold the dynamic character of our life and society from the depth of vision of Truth, Beauty and Goodness and not from the ukase of utilitarianism. Let education be geared to cultivation of socio-mystic efflorescence of each and every learner. That would be the true religion of man. Viewing religion from these perspectives of socio-aesthetics, Tagore observes, while highlighting his vision of Visva-Bharati, the centre of Indian and global socio-mystic and socio-aesthetic cohesion:

> Religious sects are formed in every country and every age owing to a diversity of historical causes. There will always be many, who, by tradition and temperament find special solace in belonging to a particualr sect; and

also there will be others who think that the finding of such solace can only be allowed as legitimate within the pale of their own. Between such, there needs must be quarrels. Making sample provisions for such invitable and interminable squabbles, can there be no wide meeting place, where all sects may gather together and forget their differences ? Has India, in her religious ideal, no such space for the common light of day and open air for all humanity ? The vigour with the sectarian fanatic will shake his head, makes one doubt it; the bloodshed which so frequently occurs for such trivial causes, makes one doubt it; the cruel and insulting distinctions between man and man which are kept alive under the sanction of region, make one doubt it. Still, in spite of all these, when I look back to India's own pure culture — in those ages when it flourished in its truth — I am emboldened to assert that it is there. Our fore fathers did spread a single pure white carpet where on all the world was cordially invited to take its seat in amity and good fellowship. No quarrel could have arisen there; for He in whose name the invitation went forth, for all time to come; was Santam, Sivan, Avaitm — the Peaceful, in the heart of all conflicts; the Good, who is revealed through all losses and sufferings; the One, in all diversities of creation. And in His name was this eternal truth declared in ancient India: *Atmavat sarvabhuteshu ya pashyati sa pashyati* — He alone sees, who sees all beings as himself.

—— Rabindranath Tagore: *The Centre of Indian Culture*, Visva-Bharati Bookshop, Calcutta. 1951. pp. 43-44.

To be a seer 'who sees all beings as himself' as Tagore

epitomises the ancient India socio-mystic viewpoints of religion is not a sudden outburst nor is it a sentimental approach to exhibitionism, but a genuine experience of inward vision enriched in living channels of communication' embracing all corners of the global society. As a matter of fact, he welcomes the aura of mystery and wonder in human growth and development which brings forth different dimensions of the socio-mystic efflorescence of man. Here is the poet's confession on his socio-mystic enlightenment through religion:

> My religion is essentially a poet's religion. Its touch comes to me through the same unseen and trackless channels as does the inspiration of my music. My religious life has followed the same mysterious line of growth as has my poetical life, somehow they are wedded to each other, and through their betrothal had a long period of ceremony, it was kept secret from me. I am not, I hope, boasting when I confess to my gift of poesy, an instrument of expression delicately responsive to the breath that comes from depth of feeling. From my infancy I had the keen sensitiveness which always kept my mind tingling with consciousness of the world around me, natural and human.
>
> I had been blessed with that sense of wonder which gives a child his right of entry into the treasure house of mystery which is in the heart of existence. I neglected my studies because they rudely summoned me away from the world around me, which was my friend and my companion, and when I was thirteen I freed myself from the clutch of an educational system that tried to keep me imprisoned within the stone-walls of lessons.

> I had a vague notion as to who or what it was that touched my heart's chords, like the infant which does not know its mother's name, or who or what she is. The feeling which I always had was a deep satisfaction of personality that flowed into my nature through living channels of communication from all sides.
>
> It was a great thing for me that my consciousness was never dull about the facts of the surrounding world. That the cloud was the cloud, that a flower was a flower, was enough because they directly spoke to me, because I could not be indifferent to them. I still remember the very moment, one afternoon, when coming back from school, I alighted from the carriage and suddenly saw in the sky, behind the upper terrace of house, an exuberance of deep, dark rain-clouds lavishing rich, cool shadows on the atmosphere. The marvel of it, the very generosity of its presence, gave me a joy which was freedom, the freedom we feel in the love of our dear friend

— Rabindranath Tagore : *The Religion of an Artist,* Visva-Bharati Bookshop, Calcutta 1953 pp. 10-11.

From a study of the poet's socio-mystic development of personality as delineated above, it is explicit that he has always a close association with his surroundings that appeal to him to the beyonding of his finer sensibilities and softer visions of life. Moreover, the world regarded by him as 'my friend and my companion' appears to him with unending promise of poignance and so he finds Truth backoning him to mingle in the society and highlight the inner essence of man-excellence beyond excellence.

Moreover, Tagore believes that the inner essence of

man crosses all the limitations of individual aims of life and merges in the finer sensibilities of the society. This is what he strongly recommends for the growth and development of man and society with reciprocal commitments of excellence beyond excellence. This allows Truth to be manifested in the the education of mutual sympathy and co-operation love and devotion. For a perfect harmony with the world of personality' as the outcome of the education of man's conciousness, Tagore urges on the stimulations of the creative spirit of man towards socio-mystic fulfilment as follows:

> There is a future for the whole which is in its growth, but in order to bring this about each unit works and dies to make room for the next worker. While the unit has the right to claim the glory of the whole, yet individually it cannot share the entire wealth that occupies a history yet to be completed.
>
> Of all creatures Man has reached that multicellular character in a perfect manner, not only in his body but in his personality. For centuries his evolution has been the evolution of a consciousness that tries to be liberated from the bounds at individual separateness and to comprehend in its relationship a wholeness which may be named Man. This relationship, which has been dimly instinctive, is ever struggling to be fully aware of itself. Physical education sought for efficiency in a perfect communication with the physical world; the evolution of Man's consciousness sought for truth in a perfect harmony with the world of personality.
>
> There are those who will say that the idea of humanity is an abstruction, subjective in character. It must be confessed that the concrete

> objectiveness of this living truth cannot be proved to its own units. They can never see its entireness from outside; for they are one with it. The individual cells of our body have their separate lives; but they never have the opportunity of observing the body as a whole with its past, present and future. If these cells have the power of reasoning (which they may have for aught we know) they have the right to argue that the idea of the body has no objective foundation in fact and though there is a mysterious sense of attraction and mutual influence running through them, these are nothing positively real; the sole reality which is provable is in the isolation of these cells made by gaps that can never be crossed or bridged.
>
> We know something about a system of explosive atoms whirling separately in a space which is immense compared to their own dimension. Yet we do not know why they should appear to us as a solid piece of radiant mineral. And if there is an onlooker who at one glance can have the view of the immense time and space occupied by innumerable human individuals engaged in evolving a common history, the positive truth of their solidarity will be concretely evident to him and not the negative fact of their separateness.

-- — Rabindranath Tagore: " The Creative Spirit", *The Religion of Man,* George Allen & Unwin Limited, London, 1953. pp. 47-48.

For education to be enriched with the spirit of freedom to foster the 'union of perfect sympathy' as Tagore visualizes, children must be allowed to nurture their freshness of senses to be 'vitally savage and mentally civilized'

How can this happen through education? How can education be a perennial component for acceleration of socio-mystic fulfilment? As Tagore advises, let there be the fulfilment of freedom of consciousness through education. Let education play a significant role in the life of the learner to enter deep into the infinite mystery of the sky, the light, the stars, the earth with all its multidimensional aroma. Let the learner enjoy and discover himself in the midst of the boundless mystery and suspense in and around him and fulfil the urge for knowing Truth derived from the rich experience of sympathy and co-operation. Let the diverse channels of communication derive inspiration from a posittive approach to education for efflorescence of simplicity and harmony in the exercise of freedom. Let the beauty of the inner man—the man unknown be in perfect effulgence through living channels of communication derived from exercise of freedom. As Tagore significantly observes:

> Freedom in the mere sense of independence has no content, and therefore, no meaning. Perfect freedom lies in a perfect harmony of relationship, which we realize in this world not through our response to it in knowing, but in being. Objects of knowledge maintain an infinite distance from us who are the knowers. For knowledge is not union. Therefore the further world of freedom awaits us there where we reach truth, not through feeling it by our senses or knowing it by our reason, but through the union of perfect sympathy.
>
> Children with the freshness of their senses come directly to the intimacy of this world. This is the first great gift they have. They must accept it naked and simple and must never again lose their power of immediate communication with it. For our perfection we have to be vitally savage and mentally civ-

> lized; we should have the gift to be natural with nature and human with human society. My banished soul sitting in the civilized isolation of the town-life cried within me for the enlargement of the horizon of its comprehension. I was like the torn-away line of a verse, always in a state of suspense, while the other line, with which it rhymed and which could give it fullness, was smudged by the mist away in some undecipherable distance. The inexpensive power to be happy, which, along with other children, I brought to this world, was being constantly worn away by friction with the brick-and-motar arrangement of life, by monotonously mechanical habits and the customary code of respectability.

—— Rabindranath Tagore: " The Teacher", *The Religion of Man*, George Allen & Unwin Ltd, London, 1953. pp. 172-173

The education of being rather than the education of becoming is the most significant factor in Tagore's approach to education for socio-mystic fulfilment. For such an education, what is of utmost importance, as he strongly advocates, the elimination of the 'ready-made' and exploration of the learner's capacity 'through surprises of achievement'. Education must bring forth in the learner a certain spirit of sensitiveness which would definitely inspire him to the inmost call of reality. When Tagore adorns and endears simplicity in way of life and in education, he essentially directs our attention to foster deeper human relationship in the society through individual creative and socio-mystic advancement. His own experimentations at the different educational institutions founded by him at Visva-Bharati bear the stamp of this background:

> The primary object of an institution should not be merely to educate one's limbs

and mind to be in efficient readiness for all emergencies, but to be in perfect tune in the symphony of response between life and world, to find the balance of their harmony which is wisdom. The first important lesson for children in such a place would be that of improvization, the constant imposition of the ready-made having been banished from here. It is to give occasions to explore one's capacity through surprises of achievement. I must make it plain that this means a lesson not in simple life, but in creative life. For life may grow complex, and yet if there is a living personality in its centre, it will still have the unity of creation; it will carry its own weight in perfect grace, and will not be a mere addition to the number of facts that only goes to swell a crowd.

I wish I could say that I had fully realized my dream in my school. I have only made the first introduction towards it and have given an opportunity to the children to find their freedom in Nature by being able to love it. For love is freedom; it gives us that fulness of existence which saves us from paying with our soul for objects that are immensely cheap. Love lights up this world with its meaning and makes life feel that it has that "enough" everywhere which truly is its "feast". I know men who preach the cult of simple life by glorifying the spiritual merit of poverty. I refuse to imagine any special value in poverty when it is a mere negation. Only when the mind has the sensitiveness to be able to respond to the deeper call of reality is it naturally weaned away from the lure of the fictitious value of things. It is callousness which robs us of our simple power to enjoy, and dooms us to the indignity of a

> snobbish pride in furniture and the foolish burden of expensive things. But the callousness of asceticism pitted against the callousness of luxury is merely fighting one evil with the help of another, inviting the pitiless demon of the desert in place of the indiscriminate demon of the jungle.
>
> I tried my best to develop in the children of my school the freshness of their feeling for Nature, a sensitiveness of soul in their relationship with their human surroundings, with the help of literature, festive ceremonials and also the religious teaching which enjoins us to come to the nearer presence of the world through the soul, thus to gain it more than can be measured — like gaining an instrument in truth by bringing out its music.
>
> –*Ibid*. pp. 178-180.

What Tagore actually suggests for the role of education for socio-mystic fulfilment is to bring out the inner music with which every learner is gifted. Let the Good, Beautiful and True within every learner be allowed to have their unending manifestation in diverse avenues of unique endeavour. Let him react with intense vision of the beyonding within him for a harmony of human relationship in the society. In this sense, Tagore fully justifies the theory of education as set forth by Prof. J. Welton:

> The theory of education we are attempting, to set forth is one which assumes that the activities of life should be evaluated according to a spiritual standard which finds the highest good of man in the perfection of his spritual nature — in mobility of heart and mind, in reverence and awe in the contemplation of the divine

> perfection, in love of all that is great and good, in hearty acceptance of duty, in strenuous endeavour, in earnest longing for truth, in appreciation of beauty, in an estimate of the things of life consistent with the view that what a man is far outweighs what he was, whether of material or of intellectual possessions.

— J. Welton; *"What do we mean by Education?* Macmillan & Co. London. 1915. P-93.

Undeniably,, Tagore enriches the socio-mystic poignance of education to the height of beyonding of consciousness — to a *Samadhi* of endless dimensions. Then alone, the identity of God, as he spells out, is available:

> It is widely known in India that there are individuals who have the power to attain temporarily the state of *Samadhi,* the complete mergin of the self in the infinite, a state which is indescribable. While accepting their testimony as true, let us at the same time have faith in the testimony of others who have felt a profound love, which is the intense feeling of union, for a Being who comprehends in himself all things that are human in knowledge, will and action. And he is God, who is not merely a sum total of facts, but the goal that lies immensely beyond all that is comprised in the past and the present.

— Rabindranath Tagore: *The Religion of Man,* George Allen & Unwin Ltd. London. 1953. P. 206.

Do we believe ?

6

EDUCATION FOR CREATIVE APPRECIATION AND SOCIAL CHANGE

TAGOREAN EXPERIMENTS

Education is an inner involvement always unique in nature. It is an unending challenge within for the best emancipation of man as 'men' and *viceversa*. It is an enternal askance within to discover and rediscover oneself for the well-being of others and for elimination of the little self for the cause of the greater self — the social, universal and the altruistic self.

Unlike other social thinkers of his time, Rabindranath Tagore innovates the social upbringing of a child by means of education for cultivation of creative appreciation and channelizing that education towards a conscious and creative approach to the onward march of the society in the most profound and practical manner. Here the education of learner is not merely learning by rot or 'parrot's training' but learning in joy through a living contact with Nature and society. The joy and freedom of learning as he encompasses in his experimentations and education for creative consciousness and social emancipation is a characteristc point of departure in innovations and experimentations on education for soical change.

Admittedly, Tagore is more often than not misunderstood and misappreciated for his experimentations on education for creativity and social change as these two aspects are even now wrongly considered to be poles apart, and as such, single-minded endeavour and untiring devotion to synchronization of these two mutually interdependent aspects of human development have been unusually looked at askance and even derided by the so-called intelligentsia. Who ignores that in the ukase of national struggle for independence and movement for national education, his educational thoughts and experiments at Visva-Bharati specially for socio-creative regeneration of humanity are not at all appropriately evaluated even now? Perhaps Tagore himself is responsible for such an appalling passivity and irresponsibility as he never cares for blame or appreciation *sans* an endless indepth vision for education for socio-creative emancipation. That education for joy and creativity makes healthy inroads between man and man or between man and society bears evidence from his own invaluable statement on art and creativity:

> The great use of education is not merely to collect facts, but to know men and make oneself known to man. It is the duty of every human being to master, at least to some extent, not only the language of intellect, but also that personality which is the language of Art. It is a great world of reality for man, vast and profound, the growing world of his own creative nature. This is the world of Art. To be brought up in ignorance of it is to be deprived of the knowledge and use of that great inheritance of

> humanity, which has been growing and waiting for every one of us from the beginning of our history. It is to remain deaf to the eternal voice of Man, that speaks to all men the messages that are beyond speech. From the educational point of view we know Europe where it is scientific, or at best literary. So our notion of its modern culture is limited within the boundary lines of grammar and laboratory. We almost completely ignore the aesthetic life of man, leaving it uncultivated, allowing weeds to grow there. Our newspapers are prolific, our meeting places are vociferous; and in them we wear to shreds the things we have borrowed from our English teachers. We make the air dismal and damp with the tears of our grievances. But where our arts, which, like the outbreak of spring flowers, are the spontaneous overflow of our deeper nature and spiritual mangnificence?

—— Rabindranath Tagore: "An Eastern University", *Creative Unity*, Macmillan Co.Ltd. London 1962, pp. 196-198.

To foster the creative spirit of the learner side by side with the socio-aesthetic efflorescence in him, Tagore himself makes experimentations in his own school, *Siksha-Satra*, christened by him as "The poet's school", where his primary emphasis is to impart the education for creative, communicative, joyous, corporate and thrilling living. This would ensure education for living in fulness. He, therefore, fillips nursling of pupils' sense of curiosity as a positive sign of socio-creative and socio-aesthetic consciousness. As he explicity states:

> The aim of *Siksha-Satra* is, through experience in dealing with the over-flowing abundance of child-life, its charm and simplicity, to provide

> the utmost liberty, within the surroundings that are filled with the creative possibilities with opportunites for the joy of play—the reaping of succession of novel experiences, to give the child freedom of growth which the young tree demands for its tender shoot, that field of self-expression in which all young life finds both training and experiences.

—— *The Visva-Bharati Bulletin*, Visva-Bharati, 1928. No. 9.

How does Rabindranath synchronize education for creativity and education for social development? What are his own strategies to orient pupils to such creative vision as would ably contribute to their social consciousness? What experimentations did he actually launch in his own school, *Siksha-Satra*? A study on the activities and process of learning by pupils there in the earlier years of experimentations on education for social consciousness reveals the following:

> Records are kept and reports and accounts are written up, revised and corrected giving scope for literary training in its most interesting form. Geology becomes the fertility of the plot; chemistry the use of lime and manures of all kinds of spray and disinfectants; physics the use of tools, pumps, the study of water-lift and oil engines; entomology the control of plant pests (ants, caterpillars, beetles) and diseases (leaf curl, wilt, bacterial attacks); orinthology, the study of birds in their relation first to the garden plot and to the world in general.
>
> There is no room in Siksha-Satra for Naturestudy as an abstract subject, divorced from life and the needs of life. In life the child has to face the mosquito mightily, perhaps the bug

> or flea, the bacterial of typhoid, of cholera, of small-pox as well as forces of nature which attack his trees, his plants, and his livestock. Nature-study is thus transformed into the study of nature in relation to life and daily experiences of life.

—— L. K. Elmhirst: *Rabindranath Tagore: Pioneer in Education*, John Murry, London, 1961. pp. 73-74.

When Tagore speaks on creativity in education, he also aims at education for worthwhile socialization. As a matter of fact, the ideal relationship between the teacher and the taught that he introduces in his own educational institutions at Visva-Bharati is based on an endless pursuit of creativity and critical thinking which has its deep roots in the society. So every act of creative pursuit is primarily geared to social change and social consciousnesss for the better accent of man as 'men'

Education as Tagore introspects, must be dynamic and meaningful to the society. It must teach the learner how to live in fulness so that the society in which he lives must be complimented with the rich fruits of curiosity and inward vision. A living mind which is an outcome of living education makes newer inroads to social awakening and unites man with man for a more profound and more thrilling promise of perfection. In his treatise on the education at Santiniketan, Tagore spells out the role of the living mind for a living society as follows:

> It is absence of curiosity that indicates the passivity of the mind. Today the nations dominating over the world have exhibited their indomitable curiosity upon everything of this world. There is neither any country nor any time nor, again, any subject towards which their mind is not being thrust forward. This

living power of mind on their part came out victorious throughout the world.

* * * *

The education of the Ashram is to live in fulness. One can ascend the highest peak of the first class in the examination even with a dead mind. We are regularly accustomed to this fact in our country. It is seen that the very good students of the college secure titles of honour but never secure the world. From the very beginning, I had the resolution that the boys of the Ashram would remain curious of having immediate relations all around. They will seek, examine and collect. Here teachers whose visions spread beyond the horizon of books would assemble.

—— Rabindranath Tagore: "Ashramer Siksha", *Siksha*, Visva-Bharati, 1973. pp. 248-249.

[Translated by me.

It is, indeed, known to all that Tagore has invited teachers of creative vision, who have taken the arduous task of real socialization of the pupils at Santiniketan to be true to themselves and to the global society. The motto that even now works in Visva-Bharati in all her creative programmes is to endear the philosophy of altruism and the serene vision of socio-aesthetics: *A no bhadra kratava yantu Viswatah* — let noble thoughts come to our mind from every direction.

The open vastness and the infinite sky of Santiniketan bring forth the sense of wonder and the promise of poignance for every one to strive endlessly for efflorescence of Truth, Beauty and Goodness in man and society. The functions and festivals of Visva-Bharati 'Where,' as Tagore solemnly declares, 'the world makes its home in a single nest' not only broaden the mind and widen the world of the creative curiosity of every teacher and the taught here but also make room for a happy reunion and exchange of ideas and ideals of the One Big Family of the Global Society. Admittedly, Tagore for the first time proves the fact that social reorientation of values and philosophy can be brought about by means of devotion to creative and performing arts like dance, drama, music, fine arts, etc. which disseminate the fact that real education always encapsulates the thrill and the joy of living and exercise of freedom for creativity and social excellence of mankind. As an unparalleled creative and social visionary he explains the creative ideal not as an individual's flight of emotion or sentimentalism bereft of detachment of the self but a living social and altruistic experience which brings forth contentment and joy in the contentment and joy of others. In fact, beauty and joy derived from creative consciousness are as he characteristically elucidates, the profound expressions of reality which emancipate the society from petty temptations:

> It may be said that in pictorial and other arts there are some designs that are purely decorative and apparently have no living and inner ideal to express. But this cannot be true. These decorations carry the emotional motive of the artist, which says: 'I find joy in my creation; it is good' All the language of joy is beauty It is necessary to note, however, that joy is not a pleasure, and beauty and mere pretiness. Joy is the outcome of detachment from self and lives in freedom of spirit. Beauty is that profound expression of reality which statisfies our hearts without any other allurements but its own ultimate value. When in some pure moments of ecstasy we realise this is the world around us, we see the world, not as merely existing, but as decorated in its forms, sounds, colours and lines; we feel in our hearts that

> there is One who through all things proclaims:
> 'I have joy in my creation'.

—+— Rabindranath Tagore: "The Creative Ideal", *Creative Unity*, Macmillan & Co., Ltd. London 1962 p.36.

To cultivate creativity and, for that end in view, social consciousness is to cultivate living humanity. This living humanity is undergoing severe stress and strain in a profession biased society. Professionalism has already eaten up the creative vitalities of man. As a unique foreseer of the maladies of professionalism in the global society, Tagore warns against erosion of individuality which is the positive outcome of freedom of creative consciousness. He refers to the ancient Indian Society where professionalism yoked in social regulations was not allowed to overpower individual creative freedom. In his own experimentations on education at Visva-Bharati he bids farewell to professionalism so much so that creative personalities like Nandlal Bose, Ramkinkar Beiz, Ajit Chakrabarti, Kalimohan Ghosh, Bidhusekhar Shastri, Kshitimohan Sen, Haricharn Bandyopadhyay, Nityanandabenode Goswami, Benode Behari Mukhopadhya, Santidev Ghose, Satyajit Ray have enjoyed their world of creative freedom unhindered by professional allurements. Tagore's own views are significant:

> The peoples, being living personalities, must have their self-expression, and this leads to their distinctive creations. These creations are literature, art, social symbols and ceremonials. They are like different dishes at one common feast. They add richness to our enjoyment and understanding of truth. They are making the world of man fertile of life and variedly beautiful.
>
> But the nations do not create, they merely produce and destroy. Organisations for pro-

duction are necessary. But when, actuated by greed and hatred, they crowd, away into a corner the living man who creates, then the harmony is lost, and the people's history runs at a breakneck speed towards some final catastrophe.

Humanity, where it is living, is guided by inner ideals; but where it is a dead organisation it becomes impervious to them. Its building process is only an external process, and in its response to the moral guidance it has to pass through obstacles that are gross and non-plastic.

Man as a person has his individuality, which is the field where his spirit has its freedom to express itself and to grow. The professional man carries a rigid crust around him which has very little variation and hardly any elasticity. This professionalism is the region where men specialise their knowledge and organise their power, mercilessly elbowing each other in their struggle to come to the front. Professionalism is necessary, without doubt; but it must not be allowed to exceed its healthy limits, to assume complete mastery over the personal man, making him narrow and hard, exclusively intent upon pursuit of success at the cost of his faith in ideals.

In ancient India professions were kept within limits by social regulation. They werre considered primarily as social necessities, and in the second place as the means of livelihood for individuals. Thus man, being free from the constant urging of unbounded competition, could have leisure to culture his nature in its completeness.

—*Ibid*, pp. 144-146

Being emancipated from bare competition affecting creative and social fulfilment, education must make ample room for understanding and appreciation of health and warm relationship between man and man. Tagore, therefore, advises us to approach education to foster the gradual emancipation of man from 'I am' to Thou art , from the finite to the infinite world of socio-creative consciousness. This would lead us to attain the real joy, the living truth that sustains humanity. This would allow the reality of oneness so heavily distorted in a seek, hurry and divided world today. That man's existence is entirely dependent on this socio-creative vision is remarkably suggested by Tagore as follows:

> That fact that we exist has its truth in the fact that every thing else does exist, and the "I am" in me crosses its finitude whenever it deeply realizes itself in the "Thou art". This crossing of the limit produces joy, the joy that we have in beauty, in love, in greatness. Self-forgetting, and in a higher degree, self-sacrifice, is our acknowledgement of this, our experience of the infinite. This is the philosophy which explains our joy in all arts, the arts that in their creations intensity the sense of the unity which is the unity of truth we carry within ourselves. The personality in me is a self-conscious principle of a living unity; it at once comprehends and yet transcends all the details of facts that are individually mine, my knowledge, feeling, wish and will, my memory, my hope, my love, my activities, and all my belongings. This personality which has the sense of *One* in its nature, realizes it in things, thoughts and facts made into units. The principle of unity which it contains is more or less perfectly satisfied in a beautiful face or a picture, a poem, a song, a character or a harmony of inter-related ideas or facts and then for if these things become in-

> tensely real, and therefore joyful. Its standard of reality, the reality that has its perfect revelation in a perfection of harmony, is hurt when there is a consciousness of discord—because discord is against the fundamental unity which is in its centre.

—— Rabindranath Tagore: *The Religion Of An Artist*, Visva-Bharati Bookshop, Calcutta 1953. pp. 15-16.

When Tagore accelerates experimentations on education for creative appreciation, he intends to bring forth the sense of the infinite feeling of joy and freedom which abundantly contributes to the harmony of socio-creative consiciousness of the learner. He allows freedom of creativity and critical thinking to the teacher and the taught only to be self-disciplined in every form of interaction within himself and in the society to which he belongs. To have faith in freedom is as he strongly advocates, to have faith in creative which allows the learner to be flexible and elastic to every form of idea or experience—social, individual, creative, etc. Whatsoever. Let the living spirit of creativity and social experience be wedded together to welcome the new-born baby of the beyonding of socio-creative consciousness in an enlightened world of our very own. Elucidating the spirit of freedom, Tagore observes:

> By squeezing human beings in the grip of an inelastic system and forcibly holding them fixed, we have ignored the laws of life and growth. We have forced living souls into a permanent passivity, making them incapable of moulding circumstance to their own intrinsic design, and of mastering their own destiny. Borrowing our ideal of life from a dark period of our degeneracy, we have covered up our sensitiveness of soul under the immovable weight of a remote past. We have set up an elaborate ceremonial of cage-worship, and plucked all

the feathers from the wings of the living spirit of our people. And for us, — with our centuries of degradation and insult, with the amorphousness of our national unity, with our helplessness before the attack of disasters form without and our unreasoning self-obstructions from within, — the punishment has been terrible. Our stupefaction has become so absolute that we do not even realise this persistent misfortune, dogging our steps for ages, cannot be a mere accident of history, removable only by another accident from outside.

Unless we have faith in freedom, knowing it to be creative, manfully taking all its risks, not only do we lose the right to claim freedom in politics, but we also lack the power to maintain it with all our strength. For that would be like assigning the service of God to a confirmed atheist. And men, who contemptuously treat their own brothers and sisters as eternal babies, never to be trusted in the most trivial details of their personal life, — coercing them at every step by the cruel threat of persecution into following a blind lane leading to nowhere, driving a number of them into hypocrisy and into moral inertia, — will fail over and over again to rise to the height of their true and severe responsibility. They will be incapable of holding a just freedom in politics, and of fighting in freedom's cause.

—— Rabindranath Tagore: "The Spirit of Freedom" *Creative Unity,* Macmillan & Co. Ltd., London, 1962. pp. 138-140.

Very often misunderstood by chivalrous intelligentsia waving the banner of the freedom of nothingness *sans* ukase in all-round affairs of life, Tagore wants to crystallize the spirit of freedom in the spirit of creativity and social excellence. Not by running riot in so-called modernity in education, but essentially being true to the age-old Indian spirit of *Santam, Sivam, Advaitam,* he incorporates the idea and exercise of creative education in the ashramic life of Santiniketan where children respond to the diverse beckonings of Nature with all her infinite aura of mystery and wonder. The depth of vision thus nourished in a sylvan atmosphere of erudition and edification of man prepares and assures mankind for a promise of social responsibility which as he proves, cannot be translated directly through overjealous and romantic aping of modernism but through a serene synthesis of contemplation and action, involvement and devotion, alas, sadly missing in the melee of automation and passivity in education. Indeed, we have lost sight of the Tagorean philosophy education for living creative appreciation and social excellence.

With a broader vision of education for creative appreciation and social change as Tagore promotes through Visva-Bharati it would be possible for us to rediscover the role of India for true global harmony and for that end in view, the horizon of individual excellence. As he poignantly suggests:

> What is evident in this world is the end less procession of moving things; but what is to be realized is the supreme human Truth by which the human world is permeated.
>
> We must never forget today that a mere movement is not valuable in itself, that it may be a sign of dangerous form of inertia. We must be reminded that a great upheaval of spirit, a universal realization of true dignity of man once caused by Buddha's teachings in India, started a movement for centuries which produced illumination of literature, art, science and numerous efforts of public beneficance.

> This was a movement whose motive force was not some addition of exceptional accession of knowledge or power or urging of some overwhelming passion. It was an inspiration for freedom, the freedom which enables us to realize *dharma,* the truth of Eternal Man.
>
> * * * *
>
> Progress which is not related to an inner *dharma,* but to an attraction which is external, seeks to satisfy our endless claims. But civilization, which is an ideal, gives us the abundant power to renounce which is the power that realizes the infinite and inspires creation.

—— Rabindranath Tagore: "Man's Nature" *The Religion of Man,* George Allen & Unwin Ltd., London. 1953. pp. 154-155.

The finer elements of social and creative excellence await translation in real life situation and education cannot but cater to individual freedom of creative appreciation for the ultimate enrichment of humanism. Tagore encourages a wider expansion of creative consciousness in his educational experimentations at Visva-Bharati so that the learner in course of his spontaneous and living association with different functions and festivals througthout the year can realize the truth of the Eternal Man awaiting fulness of manifestation.

How does education pave avenues for emancipation of man through creative and socio-aesthetic vision? How is the Eternal Man manifested in fulness of life and action ? For Tagore, education is an unending process of refinement of vision till the learner is in unison with the Eternal Man within him awaiting efflorescence in diverse dimensions. Therein lies the joy of learning through contemplation or through involvement in joyous activities. That is true freedom. That is emancipation of individuality in creative consciousness for action. Tagore makes a fine analysis of work from the socio-creative poignance of vision:

> The more a man is doing work, the more is he turning out visible whatsoever is invisible within his own self. The more is he bringing the distant future nearer. In this way man is continually making himself distinct: He is visualizing himself from different directions in manifold activities of his own, in the state, in the society.
>
> This very visualization is freedom. Darkness is not freedom nor is it absence of clarity. There is no more fearful constraint than vagueness. To come out of all indistinctness is the endeavour of the seedling out of the seed, that of the flower out of the bud. With a view to blooming effectively by tearing off the veil of vagueness, the ideas inherent in our mind is seeking avenues of efflorescence outside. Our soul, too, is continually creating activities so that it might bring itself outside by making it free from the mist of abstraction. Even the action unnecessary for him or not needed for leading his life is undergoing continual orientation by him. This is because he wants freedom. He wants freedom from his inner covering. He wants freedom from the veil of the invisible within him. He wants to see himself, have himself. The beauty that he emancipates out of ugliness at the time of making a garden by clearing off the bushes, is the beauty inherent in himself, which fails to have freedom within *sans* freedom from outside. The goodness that he allows emancipation out of the constraints of evil by establishing good rules amidst social indiscipline is the inherant goodness in him. If it is not allowed freedom from outside, it fails to achieve

freedom from within.

—— Rabindranath Tagore: "Karmayog", "Santiniketan," *Rabindra-Rachanavali,* Government of West Bengal, Calcutta. Tagore Birth Centenary Edition, 1961. Vol. XII. pp. 385-386.

[Translated by me.

The goodness in action that Tagore inspires us to seek in devotion to social and creative activities is the odyssey of our education for inward excellence. The truth of that excellence lies in the cohesion of inward vision. Not to thrive one's own consciousness of the mind alone but to apply oneself, to submit oneself and so reward oneself by others in and around oneself--this, then, should be the outcome of education for creative appreciation. On the cross-roads of extinction of humanity and creativity, in the bewildering atmoshpere of parasitism and passivity, and in the scoffing spirit of abstraction and denial, let us be baptised with Tagore's vision of paradise to unfold Truth, appreciate the creative soul and listen to the heart of life — the song of serene infinity. Let each of us, being christened as an artist as above, follow the role of an artist in the true spirit of socio-creative excellence and beyond of man :

> When the man-made world is less an expression of man's creative soul than a mechanical device for some purpose of power, then it hardens itself, acquiring proficiency at the cost of the subtle suggestiveness of living growth. In his creative activities man makes Nature instinct with his own life and love. But with his utilitarian energies he fights Nature, banishes her from his world, deforms and defiles her with the ugliness of his ambitions.
>
> This world of mans's own manufacture, with its discordant shrieks and swagger, impresses on him the scheme of a universe

which has no touch of the person and therefore no ultimate significance. All the great civilizations that have become extinct must have come to their end through expression of humanity; through parasitism on a gigantic scale bred by wealth, by man's clinging reliance on material resources; through a scoffing spirit of denial, of negation, robbing us of our means for sustenance in the path of truth.

* * * *

I believe that the vision of Paradise is to be seen in the sunlight and the green the earth, in the beauty of the human face and the wealth of human life, even in objects that are seemingly insignificant and unprepossessing. Everywhere in this earth the spirit of Paradise is awake and sending forth its voice. It reaches our inner ear without our knowing it. It tunes our harp of life which sends our aspiration in music beyond the finite, not only in prayers and hopes, but also in temples which are flames of fire in stone, in pictures which are dreams made everlasting, in the dance which is ecstatic meditation in the still centre of movement.

—— Rabindranath Taogre : *The Religion of An Artist*, Visva-Bharati Bookshop, Calcutta. 1953. pp. 26-27.

Are we really involving ourselves in the odyssey of such serene illumination and poignance to a new human destiny?

Index